A La Recherche du Cricket Perdu

SIMON BARNES

MACMILLAN
LONDON

First published 1989 by
MACMILLAN LONDON LIMITED
4 Little Essex Street London WC2R 3LF
and Basingstoke

Associated companies in Auckland, Delhi, Dublin, Gaborone,
Hamburg, Harare, Hong Kong, Johannesburg, Kuala Lumpur,
Lagos, Manzini, Melbourne, Mexico City, Nairobi, New York,
Singapore and Tokyo

A CIP catalogue record for this book is available from the
British Library

ISBN 0-333-48722-2

Typeset by Wyvern Typesetting Ltd, Bristol
Printed and bound by WBC Ltd, Bristol and Maesteg

CONTENTS

iii

CONTENTS

INTRODUCTION

I don't understand. I just don't understand what's going off out there. The cricket writers of today just don't seem to have any idea . . .

Ah, declining standards: where would we be without them? If it is not the failure to bowl line and length or the playing of the reverse sweep, it is the declining literary standards of the cricket reports in the papers. Cardus is gone, Arlott is retired, and even Woodcock is flirting with retirement.

It was clearly time to put things right. Cricket needs a Proust, a Dante, a Shakespeare, as well as an Ian Fleming and a P. G. Wodehouse. I have tried to supply all of them myself: how's that for hubris?

I would like to thank Miles Kington, who inadvertently started me off on this project with a couple of cricket parodies of his own. I would also like to thank my wife and all my friends for listening to these pieces, and for laughing at the jokes, no matter how many times I tried them out.

A La Recherche du Cricket Perdu

MARCEL PROUST

LEICESTER: *Leicestershire, with seven second-innings wickets in hand, lead Warwickshire by 54 runs.*

For a long time I used to doze off early. Sometimes, no sooner had I taken my seat in the press-box, sometimes, indeed, before I had so much as seen that the players, whose joys and sadnesses I was required to record that day, had emerged from the pavilion, before even the umpires (whom Bloch would always refer to as 'sage judges from High Olympus sent') had placed the bails on the wickets, I would give myself up to slumber.

On these occasions, the shirts of the lithe young athletes, fitted with inordinate tightness as was the prevalent fashion, would seem somehow to lose their tautness, would insensibly commence to flow and to billow about their bodies until the players seemed clad in the silken shirts of a former age. At the crease itself, the batsman's helmet, donned, it would often seem, as much as a ritual token of respect for the manliness of his opponent as for physical protection,

3

would itself seem to soften, to lose all its protective virtue, and the bars of that harsh cage that was set to guard but which seemed in fact to imprison the features which lurked behind it, would seem to shrink to the thickness of strands of cobweb, until a sprightly gust were enough to blow it away, and the helmet itself was transformed into, say, an MCC touring cap, or a Harlequins cap as affected by Jardine or, best yet, a cap assumed by the members of the ancient and mighty Tewin Irregulars.

And as I fitfully dozed, the chairs, not designed for so peaceful a use and so refusing to permit my slumber to be anything but a troubled and fitful one, the awkward, uncoached nudges and slashes of the callow youths at the crease were transmuted into greatness by my intermittently sleeping eyes, until I saw before me cover-drives rolling in splendour from the bats long decayed and wielded by men long since dead: Hammond, whose air of languid elegance caused me almost to rejoice one afternoon at Lord's when I had repaired there after seeking Mme Swann in vain the length of the Avenue des Acacias, or even of Grace himself, within the syllables of whose name every joy and every secret of the game seem to be concealed.

As I watched, the players of the present time seemed no more substantial than ghosts, indeed, infinitely less solid than the spectres of players from the past whom the necromancy of sleep had conjured into life, wraiths that seemed far more real, far more suffused with purpose, with skill and with meaning, shades far more capable of bringing joy – the things of our youth being always more capable of bringing

4

joy than the indifferent and callous present, as, indeed, they are infinitely more capable of bringing tears – than any of the helmeted men of today, so much so that these ranks of remembered cricketers seemed to align themselves before me, one generation alongside the next, reaching into the distant past of my childhood and stretching as far as the present day, until the field became crowded with untold numbers of cricketers, and a thousand bowlers ran in at once to release their missiles with a thousand variations of ferocity and guile, while a thousand batsmen, short, tall, languid, hurried, burly or elegant, similar only in the mightiness of the places they occupied in my memory, stood together in one long unbroken line to defy all the bowlers of history and to despatch, perhaps with grace or perhaps with savage, ghostly strength, the spectral bowlers' finest efforts, and send them soaring away, out of sight, and out of memory once again.

One wakes, unsure in which press-box one sits, unsure even of the decade in which one is watching, perplexed at the sudden blow that has in a single instant reduced this vast army of cricketers to a mere thirteen. And then one notes that Gower, the theatricality of whose stroke-making always recalls Berma in one of her classic roles (the reputation of which causes so painful a scene to be enacted by M. de Norpois), had struck 54 runs, but had been dismissed with the last ball before tea. Ah, tea! I could, I think, find a great deal to write about within a cup of tea, were it not that cricket is so much more redolent of things past.

Moby Quick

HERMAN MELVILLE

LORD'S: *Hampshire beat Middlesex by ten wickets.*

Call me Wooders. Some years ago I joined a cricket team, to drive off the spleen and to see the green part of the world. Being the meanest of my sort, I was required to do the will not only of one Captain Gatt, but also of all other members of my side. This is not an easy thing for a grand sort of fellow to do; but look at it judgmatically. Who ain't a team-mate, playing for some greater captain? Who ain't full of duties of all kinds to all sorts of other men?

In truth Captain Gatt spoke little to me. He spoke little to any man. He would pace about the little dressing room, with a grim aspect and a barbaric red patch which he wore where his nose once stood. Hour after hour, he would pace the room's length, till you wondered at the distance he might have travelled. One day, before a game, he seemed to pace harder than ever. It drew close to the start. Suddenly he came to a halt, and ordered the entire team to stand before him. With curious and apprehensive faces we gathered at his corner nearest the showers, and at once, he cried –

'What do we do to a batsman, men?'

'Get him out!'

'How do we get him out, men?'

'Knock his head off!'

'Aye, aye, now look ye. Ye see this? 'Tis a sponsor's cheque. Now then, Embers, nail it to the dressing room door. 'Twill go to the man who knocks the head off the great black bowler, my boys!'

'Huzza! Huzza!' we cried, as Embers pinned the cheque to the door.

'Captain Gatt,' said Embers. 'That black bowler must be the same that some call Moby Quick.'

'Aye, aye! Death and devils, aye! 'Tis Moby Quick, I tell thee.'

'Captain Gatt,' said Embers. 'I have heard of Moby Quick. Was it not Moby Quick that took off thy nose? And is not that patch on thy face made from the very ball with which he dismasted thee?'

'Who told thee that?' cried Gatt. 'Aye, Embers, aye me hearties all round, it was Moby Quick, Moby Quick that made a poor noseless lubber of me. So shall I be until the day I die. But today we shall have him. I think ye do look brave! And 'tis against Moby Quick we bat this very morning in the Benson and Hedges Cup!'

There is no place in the world so jolly as a cricket dressing room before an innings of vast dangers. Old enmities are sunk, old jokes are recalled, old songs are sung. For we know that the profound walk out from the pavilion to bat is more dreadful than batting itself, though we be struck six times in an over.

But why labour the matter? All men are facing the bowling of the most fearsome attack in the world

7

every day of their lives. Any moment that you spend may bring the delivery that ends your innings. It is not that cricketers live imperilled lives, for is not every one of us forever waiting for the head-ball that comes and which shall not be evaded? Thus those caught in the swift, sudden turns of cricket know that every living moment is moored hard by the bark of death. The philosophical man knows that he spends every moment of his life in as much proximity to eternity and with as great a certainty of death as any cricketer that every played, though he work at a desk, not a wicket, and with a Filofax, not a cricket bat, in his hand.

A Game to the Music of Time

ANTHONY POWELL

Cricket grounds seem inescapably imbued with melancholy, perhaps because they remind one too forcibly of the vast tracts of gloom associated with one's schooldays, and with the laborious, indeed, well-nigh baroque contrivances one employed to escape the duties of playing cricket for one's house.

But somehow that day I was conscious of an un-usually increased sense of unease, a feeling connected, for some reason, with a banana laid on an adjacent desk in the press-box: large; over-ripe; scrofulous; apparently part of the lunch brought by a colleague from the Press Association. On encountering this sight, my thoughts drifted to Widmerpool, and to the monstrous figure he used to cut when playing cricket, wearing his uncommonly thick spectacles, through the glass windows of which he was accustomed to survey his unattainable sporting goals with such peevish intensity.

Then I recalled the way in which Widmerpool and fruit were always linked in my mind: it was at Wid-merpool's face that a banana had been pitched on that famous occasion at school, later recounted to me by Stringham as we took tea together. Stringham had laid great stress on the 'slavish expression' on Widmerpool's face as he received the apologies of the thrower. This had been Budd, the captain of the Eleven. Widmerpool's delight in being noticed by so great a person as Budd, despite his features being liberally covered with fructuous debris, had seemed in a sense reasonable: grotesque only in so far as anything Widmerpool did was irredeemably associated with the grotesque.

Musing on this matter, I left the press-box and elected to take a turn around the ground. At one point, near the pavilion, my way was blocked. A figure, tall, not without grace, and dressed in cricketing whites, clearly a member of the batting side not yet called on to perform, was standing in the path, apparently lost in thought. I asked him to move: he leapt aside with a sudden, almost guilty air, and turned to me to offer an apology. It was Budd.

'Why, Budd, I didn't know you were a professional cricketer.'

'All the same, I am.'

He appeared to consider this a reply of unusual neatness, giving me at the same time a smile which displayed what Stringham called 'those film-star teeth'. He looked more than ever like the hero of an adventure story for boys.

'How do you enjoy being a cricketer?'

'Very much indeed.' He added, in a perceptibly deeper, and quieter tone: 'It's the people, you know.' He seemed to imply that his intimacies with 'the

people' were something questionable, slightly sham-
ing, possibly even indecent.

'You don't find the game palls when it becomes a
job?'

'Well, I also work for a sports goods firm. I work for
the company that manufactures sports shoes in the
Balkans and sells them here.' He named the country
once ruled by Prince Theodoric.

'Isn't that a firm run by Widmerpool – Widmerpool
who was in Le Bas's house?'

'That's right. As a matter of fact, it was Widmerpool that gave me the job. The firm sponsors the
county, you know. In fact, Widmerpool was uncommonly helpful when my contract came up for renewal
in the winter. He has a lot of weight around here, you
know, though no official position. I think he wanted
someone reliable on the players' committee, and so
persuaded the county that it was in their best interests
to keep me on, despite my poorish form over the past
couple of seasons.'

'That was good of him.'

'Widmerpool is not one to forget an old friend.'

Life seems sometimes to consist of a series of violent
adjustments to radically changed circumstances. For
Budd to consider Widmerpool a friend, let alone a
friend to whom he was deeply grateful, would have
required, it would have seemed when one was at
school, the stars to start from their courses. Widmerpool then seemed doomed to be forever the butt of
jokes, and the accidental target for bananas in any
game that was played. But as we continue with the
game, the rules that seemed so clear and so immutable

at first now seem subject to continuous change and reinterpretation, so that one is no longer clear what actions one is permitted to take, and no longer possesses any clear understanding of the object of the game. Indeed, victory itself, seen once as the sole reason for the existence of the game, no longer seems attainable, or even for that matter, desirable.

How's That, Jeeves?

P. G. WODEHOUSE

I don't know if you've ever had the same experience, but I have always found that whenever I am most conspicuously full of *joie de vivre* and *espiéglerie*, it is a sign that fate is sneaking up behind me in order to sock me on the base of the skull with a cricket bat.

Right ho. Let me marshal my facts. Jeeves – the players' dressing-room attendant at Loamshire, don't you know? – had just brought me that perfect pre-match cup of tea. The bird was on the wing and, if my memory serves me correctly, there was not a cloud in the sky.

'Well,' I said. 'Here we are again, what?'

'Indeed, sir.'

'All set for a semi in the jolly old Benson and Hedges.'

'Precisely, sir.'

'And the bally weather, too – am I right, Jeeves, or am I wrong?'

'It is certainly exceedingly clement, sir. Excuse me, sir, are you proposing to play cricket in that hat?'

'What's wrong with it?'

'Oh, nothing, sir.'

'Out with it, Jeeves. You don't like this hat.'

'For fishing, or for relaxing on the beach, it would be excellent, sir.'

'It's a fielding hat, Jeeves. For fielding in.'

'If I might make the suggestion, sir, for a county captain, the county cap is more suitable.'

'Fiddlesticks, Jeeves.'

'Very good, sir.'

'Absolute blather from the sickbed.'

'As you say, sir.'

'Heaps of chaps have asked me who I bought it from.'

'Doubtless in order to avoid the man, sir.'

Well, the blood of the Woosters was stirred by this. I could see that it was time I put my foot down, if I was not to become a slave to my own dressing-room attendant. If he expected Bertram Wooster to give this hat the miss in baulk, then he expected wrong.

No one has greater respect for Jeeves's judgement than myself. I am prepared to admit that in the matter of flannels, and even of pads, he stands alone. But in my view, hats are, and have always been, his weak spot.

'Oh, by the by, Jeeves, what do you think the wicket will do today?'

'I really could not say, sir.'

I could tell that the blighter was miffed. Spurning the young master. 'That will be all, Jeeves,' I said coldly, and I meant it to sting, by God.

Jeeves shimmered off into his lair, leaving me to contemplate my fate. But I had hardly got into first gear with contemplation when our number five batsman, Gussie Fink-Nottle, burst into the room like an aspiring tornado. A small cry escaped me.

'Bertie, something ghastly has happened.'

'Oh–ah?' I replied, cordially enough. I don't know if you know Gussie – looks like a fish, sound batsman of the defensive kind, imagines he's a demon leg-spin bowler – but he is one of life's leading fatheads.

'Madeleine has broken off our engagement.'

'Gosh!' I said.

And I'll tell you why I goshed. Madeleine Bassett, telephone receptionist at Loamshire, and the fathead-est girl who ever thought that the stars were God's daisy-chain and that whenever a baby laughs a wee fairy is born, has it firmly fixed in her woollen mind that Bertram is pining away for the love of her. If she had broken it off with Gussie, then she would be at my side in a trice, expecting me to buy the licence and start ordering the cake.

'Why?' I gulped.

'She made a slighting remark about my abilities as a leg-spin bowler.'

'Oh, I say, what?'

'I couldn't bring myself to repeat it.'

'Have a bash!'

'So I told her she knew nothing about cricket, and she said she knew a sight more than I did, and that she'd sooner die than marry a man who couldn't bowl a hoop downhill.'

I made a grab for the bell. 'Jeeves!' The fellow reappeared. I explained the posish.

'Accept my condolences, Mr Fink-Nottle,' he said.

'Thank you, Jeeves.'

'Will that be all, sir?'

'But I say, Jeeves,' I blurted. 'What am I going to do?'

'No doubt a course of action will suggest itself to you, sir.'

I cast a look at my fielding hat, and I must confess, I wavered. But we Woosters have our code.

'I am sorry to have troubled you, Jeeves,' I said frostily, and he shimmered away again.

I went out to toss up with the opposing captain – did I tell you it was Surrey we were playing? – and lost. We were asked to bat. I sauntered back to the pavilion trying hard not to look like a man bowed down with care. Jeeves greeted me: 'Sir, I have been asked to impart a message to you.'

'Impart away, Jeeves.'

'Anatole, the Loamshire cook, has given in his notice.'

I began to feel rather like one that on a lonesome road that walks in fear and dread, and having once turned round walks on and turns no more his head, because he knows a fearful fiend doth close behind him tread. Anatole is a master of his art, and the most cherished cook in county cricket, the envy of every club in the country. 'But why, Jeeves?'

'He has received an offer from Surrey.'

'But, dash it, why has he accepted it?'

'He is love with Pamela, the lady who serves the drinks in the members' bar. She has also given in her notice. It was her decision to leave that prompted Anatole to follow her.'

'But why is she leaving?'

'She feels that Loamshire's failure to reach a one-day final reflects on her personal dignity.'

'But I mean to say, we might win this match and get to Lord's.'

'She is not sanguine. In fact, she was heard to liken Loamshire's chances of winning today to those of a snowball in hell.'

'Blast her!'

'Yes, sir.'

'Blast everything.'

'Very good, sir. But as the Emperor Marcus Aurelius once said, all that befalls you is part of the great web, sir.'

'Marcus Aurelius said that, did he?'

'Yes, sir.'

'Well, next time you see him, tell him he's an ass.'

'Very good, sir.'

As Jeeves once remarked, when sorrows come, they come not single spies but in battalions. Our chaps batted badly. We were all out for 150. Gussie and I both made ducks. It was frightful. It was the bally frightfulness of it all that made it all so frightfully bally.

Lunch was a torment. Anatole's food turned to ashes in my mouth. Madeleine Bassett walked through the dining room, gave Gussie a cold look, and then gave me a smile I can only describe as threatening. Jeeves said not a thing. I tell you, it was frightful.

By the tea interval, it was worse. Surrey were 110 for three with thirty overs left. I had tried all our best bowlers, and none of them had done a thing. I don't mind telling you, I was stumped.

I heard a gentle cough by my side. It was Jeeves. 'If I might make a suggestion, sir.'

'You might, Jeeves, you might.'

'I believe the wicket will be more than usually responsive to spin, sir. I suggest bowling Mr Fink-Nottle at the pavilion end.'

'Mr Fink-Nottle, Jeeves? But you know the man can't bowl to save his life.'

'I believe that this is the one wicket that will suit him, sir. I also believe that Surrey are singularly ill-suited to playing leg-spin.'

Well, if Jeeves gives you advice, you ignore it at your peril. When tea was over, we took to the field, and the first thing I did was to throw the ball to old Gussie. The sight of him running in, looking more like a fish than anything you'd ever find in a sauce Mornay, caused the batsman to grin cheerfully. He was still grinning as he attempted to smite the ball into the middle distance. He missed. The ball hit the wicket.

That was the beginning of it all. To cut a long story short, Gussie took seven wickets for 10 runs, and Surrey were beaten by 7 runs. Gussie, blushing like a modest flounder, led us off the field.

'My hero!' said *la* Bassett, as we entered the pavilion, and I gave a gusty sigh of relief and returned to the dressing room. Jeeves was there to meet me. 'Sir, I have a message for you.'

'Tell me all, Jeeves.'

'Anatole has withdrawn his notice. Pamela from the members' bar refused to go to Surrey after their performance this afternoon.'

'Wonderful.'

'Most gratifying, sir.'

'And all because of your suggestion to bowl Gussie.'

'Very kind of you to put it that way, sir.'

'No, really, Jeeves, you stand alone.'

'Thank you, sir.'

I felt a pang of regret, but I knew what had to be done. 'Jeeves, you know my fielding hat?'

'Indeed, sir.'

'Is it really so frightful?'

'A trifle inappropriate, sir.'

'Give it away, Jeeves.'

'Thank you, sir. I have already given it to the groundsman's younger son.'

'Thank you, Jeeves.'

'Not at all, sir.'

The Virgin and the All-Rounder

D. H. LAWRENCE

The scorer for Worcestershire was called Jennifer Trimble. She came from a good family – oh! such a good family. But she was dead inside, dead. Yet somehow not quite dead, not yet. Sometimes, when she recorded the scores with her meticulous pencilling, she felt some small and rebellious thing stir within her. And it was hateful to feel it, yet somehow it was more hateful still when it had gone.

It had nothing to do with the cricketers, nothing at all. They were all so very nice and so very harmless. 'They are awfully good sorts, the chaps in the team,' she would say, as she sat in her scorer's place high above the pavilion. 'But you couldn't imagine dallying with them, now could you?' And as she said it she was quite sincere, quite open about everything.

But when Mrs Gargling, the tea lady, replied: 'Aye, ah knows there's no one in't world quite good enough for thee,' she did feel most horribly hurt: hurt in her limbs, in her body, in her sex, hurt. Hurt, numbed and half-destroyed.

And one season seemed to follow another, and the

new one seemed very much like the one before. Though there would be two new players this time, a fast bowler and an all-rounder, and she was sure they would be nice chaps, nice chaps you couldn't have anything to do with really. Another season of pleasant chaps and pleasant days, and all the time feeling dead inside. But what could she do?

She arrived early on the first day, with her pencils and erasers. She was always so very neat, always so very meticulous. The cricketers were there before her, stretching and straining as they prepared for their game. She walked past them without turning her head, going to her roost, her aloof spot above the pavilion. And she heard a voice.

'Where art thou goin', lass, wi' thy rubbers and scratchlings?' It was a warm voice, like no cricketer's voice she had ever heard, and it seemed to caress her with a warm, slow heat. She turned. It was the new all-rounder, a blond giant of a man. He stood before her, curiously humble, curiously vulnerable with his small moustache and his flowing blond curls falling on to his shoulder. He was tall and broad, and somehow utterly unlike all the nice chaps she had seen play cricket before. His hair was longer, his shoulders broader. Yet it was not that that she noticed. She met his pale eyes for a second, and felt their level search, their insolence, their absolutely naked insinuation of desire.

'I'm scoring,' she said, with a silly smile.

'Oh, aye. An' 'appen ah s'll do a bit o' scorin' meself afore day is out.' And he looked at her again, with a naked insinuation of desire. He had seen none of her

pretty ways with her pencils and her erasers: just the dark, tremulous secret of her virginity.

And he slouched away to the pavilion. He had suave electric loins, he was like a pharaoh, like an Egyptian pharaoh crowned with a golden mane. And there was something dangerous about him: he was a man who never scored safe 30s, she thought. A man who dealt only in ducks and centuries. Every thought in her head warned her against such a being: yet that secret thing inside her cried out: give him to me! Give him to me! And all the while she knew it was impossible, quite impossible.

And he batted like a giant. He scorned the elegant deflections that the nice chaps played so finely: with a giant's blows he smote all that the world sent against him. His hair blond against his collar, his eyes pale and intense, he was a finely made thing that seemed to defy all that cricket's cold world could put in his way.

And when he was out for 46 a chill seemed to come into Jenny's heart. She wished to go down, to seek him out, but no, she could not do that. And then she felt a step on the stair behind her: the blond giant was beside her. Warm and alive from his mighty exertions, he sat beside her. In one hand he held his mighty bat, in the other, a small bunch of daisies.

'Oh!' she cried. 'You have some flowers.'

'Aye. An' it so 'appens ah've some very novel ideas on flower arranging, lass. Shall I show thee?'

'Yes!' said Jenny. 'Oh yes!' And something seemed to catch fire within her.

La Divina Cricketa

DANTE

THE STORY: Virgil leads Dante into the circle of Hell that contains the shades of wicked sportsmen. Dante meets one he knows and confronts him. The shade prophesies great evil for English cricket.

Editor's note: The translation is by Florence Gabrielli Smythe. We admit that her attempt at *terza rima* is pretty awful doggerel, but it is the best we could find. We considered running the poem in Italian, but we believe that Dante suffers dreadfully in the original.

And thus we reached a place where the dull
   thrumming
Was like a mighty rain and did assault the ears
And hearing. I turned to see my Master coming

And said: 'Great knowing one, I would you calmed
   the fears
That do surround me, and tell me of this
   place.
How doom enfolds it! How full of horrors it
   appears!'

And he to me: 'Step close beside, and slow your
     pace.
For this is not a time to hurry on alone.
Shades lie here, many whom you do not wish to
     face.

No hope lies here, for here all hopes are ripped and
     blown;
Here victory's joy and comfort in defeat were sold,
Team-mates betrayed. Here honest players are
     unknown.'

I began to faint, and my heart did grow less bold.
'Twas true this place would bring me those I knew
     full well.
I turned my eyes forward: what a scene there did
     unfold!

The sky was cracked with tolling of a vasty bell,
My master spoke to me with horror in his eyes:
You guessed it right: here is the sportsman's place
     in hell.

Here are the cricketers the world will long despise:
The chuckers and the sledgers, all the men who
     cheat,
Batsmen who refuse to walk, fielders who tell lies,

Bowlers who make false appeals, those who, just
     to beat
Their foe, will bend or break the custom and the
     law,

And those who the final slice of fruitcake ay will
    eat.'

I raised my eyes, and through the swirling mist I
    saw
Ten thousand sportsmen fill the air with doleful
    cries
As they lay shackled, naked, on their piles of
    gore.

They lay pegged out for ever, there between the
    walls
Of this great Circle. As they groaned, the sky
Sent down on them a horrid rain of cricket balls.

Then saw I one I knew, and I said to him: 'Why?
You were ever a great player – how came you to
    this?'
And he: 'Weep not for me! I will not have you cry.

For I am Gucci, he whom the world he loved will
    never miss.
I am here, as you must know, because I did betray
All English cricket. For that, I lie in this abyss.

For I was a Rebel, and therefore I did play
Not for England, but a foreign Brewery team.
I waxed in wealth, 'tis true, but what boots that
    today?'

I sprang forward, and with a loud voice said: 'I
    deem

You are where you should be. You who had the
   trust
Of cricket, did a nightmare make of cricket's
   dream.'

For answer, Gucci snarled: 'Be glad I am so
   trussed!
Or I would beat till you were no more alive.
Instead, I prophesy that England will be cursed.

When next against the Windies men they strive,
England, and English cricket shall fall asunder.
Of captains, one summer yields no less than five!'

Looking grave, my Master led me out and under
An arch that in the Circle's wall was nearby set.
I said: 'Be sure that Gucci makes a foolish blunder!

Five captains? No!' My Master said: 'How much
   d'you bet?'

You're Only Out Once

IAN FLEMING

The crack of the weapon striking home filled the room.

The sound was absorbed by the walls of the windowless building that had been constructed on the Schloss-Mockenbecker principle. James Bond walked back along the Hi-Bounce surface and commented: 'This one seems just about perfect, Fearnley.'

The armourer snorted. 'Come back and tell me after you've been in the middle with it, sir.'

But Bond was pleased with his new weapon. It was a twin-scooped jumbo weighing not less than four pounds, and with just the pick-up he liked. For the first time since the loss of his trusty old equaliser on his most recent assignment in the Caribbean, he felt content. And he would need to use it soon enough!

As he walked away from the indoor net, part of that anonymous cluster of buildings near Regents Park, his mind went back to the previous day. He had been faced with a pile of routine work when the red telephone in the players' dressing room had splintered the silence. 'M wants you,' the chief of staff had said urgently.

M was a man whose true function was known only to a handful of people in England. Outwardly, he seemed an ordinary businessman. But in reality, he was chairman of the selectors, who went into battle a dozen times a season with the pick of England's men. He used them as live chessmen, and spent them brutally when he had to. He would never have dreamed of telling Bond that he, Bond, was the best man he possessed.

M had been in one of his reflective moods. 'What do you think England needs?' he asked abruptly as Bond entered the room.

Bond looked into that weather-beaten face he knew so well, and which held so much of his loyalty. 'Runs in the middle order, sir,' he replied.

M flung his matchbox across the desk. 'Absolutely correct, Seven.' M would not have considered addressing Bond during the hours of play by anything other than his number in the batting order. 'And this is where you come in. I am giving you a licence to slog.'

Bond reflected on this as he sat in the England dressing room the following day. The responsibility! But it was right. England had lacked solidity in the middle order ever since Four had disappeared in the Dirty Half Mile in Pakistan. There was a scent of tension in his nostril: the lure of the big pot, the ever-present taste for the big gamble. He would do it, by God!

He stripped, gave himself a very hot and then an ice cold shower. He washed his hair with Head 'n' Shoulders, that prince of shampoos. He dressed in white trousers, and a white, Sea Island cotton shirt. He glanced at himself in the mirror: a pair of grey-blue eyes looked quizzically back at him, that rebellious comma of hair falling an inch above the right eyebrow. He brushed it back impatiently. He smiled at some memory and walked out of the dressing room on to the players' balcony. It was ten in the morning, an hour before play began.

He glanced across to the opposition players' balcony. A girl stared levelly back at him. She was very beautiful, in a devil–may–care kind of way.

She was clad in a simple white bikini. Her dark hair was thrust back from her face, her eyes cool and dark, assessed him. She sat straddling a chair, her chin on her arms. The impudent thrust of her proud breasts flayed at Bond's senses.

'Guess you're the middle–order man,' she said flatly, a hint of Australian in her voice. There was arrogance in the set of her head, in the cool shrug of her shoulders.

Bond was amused. He lit a cigarette, of the kind that Morlands of Grosvenor made specially for him, with three gold rings, and said: 'And you're the Australian fast bowler.'

She didn't smile. 'I travel with Denno, yeah.'

God, thought Bond, what a life! But something about the girl told him she was beyond that. Her eyes said: don't hurry me. All things are possible between us.

'Do you have a name?' Bond asked.

'Shirleen Sleepwell.' Her eyes held a touch of defiance.

'Nice name. I like it.'

'I'll tell Denno you said so. He'll be honoured.'

To hell with her! He, Bond had work to do. He returned to the dressing room and rang room service. 'Get me a double portion of scrambled eggs, a pint of Jack Daniel's bourbon and plenty of ice.'

'Right away, sir.'

Bond consumed his breakfast, and felt the excitement ball up inside him. This was the big play! Thank God he would soon be out in the middle.

He went to toss up with the opposition captain, won and chose to bat. The Australian offered his hand. The handshake was firm and dry. Bond smiled amiably and emptily back. He would continue to play the toothless tiger.

He returned to the dressing room and prepared himself for the battle. He watched the cricket until he was needed. He checked that the Rolex was on his wrist, and finally closed his locker. He plucked a hair painfully from his head, and with a dab of saliva stuck it across the door. He had done all he could. Now it was down to the gods. He hoped they were on his side. With the new weapon in his hand, he stepped out to do battle.

He stood at the wicket and looked across at the man he knew he would have to oppose: Denno. Denno gave the impression of being a little larger than life. He stood over six feet tall. He had an enormous head, big as a football, capped with a tangle of black curls. The left eye was not a perfect match with its fellow. The arms, preternaturally long, hung to

the level of his knees. He wore a large and astonishingly hairy moustache.

The general effect was flamboyant: like a cheap gigolo. Bond was put in mind of a cartoon braggart: a jeering loud-mouthed vulgarian. 'G'day, Jim,' Denno said. 'Are you ready for a little fun?'

'Yes,' said Bond. 'I'd like that very much.'

'I hope you've made your will,' Denno said. He retreated into the distance, the red weapon of the ball in his hand.

Bond took guard. There was something cold and dangerous in his face as Denno turned and began to run towards him. It was a tricky, almost a vicious pitch he had to play on. The odds were stacked against him. To hell with it! It was now or never.

Denno ran in and fired the ball at Bond. It was a full length, and rose abruptly to strike Bond in the ribcage. What was happening? Get up, you bastard! The pain of the impact seemed to have frozen his responses. Somehow, he scrambled to his feet. He wasn't dead yet!

'Like 'em round about there, Jim?' Denno's sneering voice penetrated his consciousness. He ignored it, concentrated only on dodging the next ball. Hit it. Hit it with anything. If not, he was a dead duck!

The second ball came, again on a length. Bond lunged blindly at it, missed, and felt a searing pain in his shoulder. Now he was done for! Not enough strength left to raise a bat! How the hell had he got mixed up with all this? He turned with infinite weariness to face the third ball.

A half-volley! Bond surged gratefully into the

drive – no, by God! A yorker! The ball struck him full on the foot, again bringing him to the ground. Denno followed the ball down the pitch. There was no stuffing left in Bond for another shouting match. He climbed the infinite distance to his feet. Counter-attack. That was his only hope!

Suddenly nothing mattered. Suddenly, the only thing that Bond wanted was to give this hairy ape the lesson of his life. The next ball was short. It was outside leg: an easy hook. Bond moved instinctively into position. Hell! It was coming straight for his head. Only one thing for it! With blind, animal desperation, Bond went through with his hook. There was a sweet, brief moment of contact, and he knew the ball was going to clear the boundary for six. That was more like it!

The second ball was shorter, faster. Bond swung again. God! Another six! Close to delirium, Bond played on towards a bloody, beckoning vortex.

Bond left the pitch, a grey-faced, lunging automaton. Somehow he had done it. A century before lunch for Number Seven. Bond felt no triumph, only a great, soul-wearying exhaustion.

He walked into the pavilion. He stripped naked and walked, almost fell into the shower. The water felt like summer rain on his back. There was a small, curiously hesitant knock on the door of the shower room.

'Who's there?' asked Bond.

'It's me – Shirleen Sleepwell. I just wondered if you had all you need.'

'Come in, Shirleen, and close the door behind you.'

She entered. She wore nothing now. 'Look here, you Bond person —'

His mouth came ruthlessly down over hers.

The Life of Swanton

JAMES BOSWELL

On Friday, 19 June, Swanton honoured me with his company at Trent Bridge. I complained that he had not mentioned Mr Denness in his piece in the newspaper that day, which was on the subject of captaincy. BOSWELL: 'Sir, you do not admire him, because he is a Scotchman. You would not praise him as you would praise an Englishman.' SWANTON: 'Why, sir, I would give him higher praise, for I would say of him, as I would not say of him were he an Englishman, that he is the finest cricket captain his country has ever produced.'

Our conversation turned upon travel. I asked him if Lahore was worth seeing. He was provoked, and answered: 'Sir, it is worth seeing, but it is not worth going to see. Indeed, sir, let me tell you that the fairest prospect which a Pakistani ever sees, is the airport at Lahore and the jumbo jet that will fly him to England.'

Mr Selvey had said to me aside, that Dr Swanton should have been a serious writer, and have written on subjects of greater importance than cricket. I repeated this remark to Swanton, that I might have his own thoughts on the subject. SWANTON: 'Sir, it would have been better that I had been a general writer.' BOSWELL:

'I do not think, sir, it would have been better, for we should not have had your daily Test match reports. Though I do not doubt you would have written as judiciously as any writer or political commentator, no writer could produce an analysis of the day's play quite in your manner.' SWANTON: 'Come, sir, that is enough. Let us drink brandy.'

There had been a women's Test match being played that week, and I, in order to draw the sage's opinions on this matter, asked him had he ever seen women's cricket. SWANTON: 'Aye, sir, once.' BOSWELL: 'Did you enjoy the spectacle, sir?' SWANTON: 'I did, sir.' BOSWELL: 'Were you impressed?' SWANTON: 'I was surprised, sir. It was like Gower bowling. It is not well done, but it is surprising to see it done at all.'

He sometimes could not bear to be teazed with questions. I asked him so many as 'How many different deliveries should a leg-spinner possess?' and 'Should a batsman always play forward or always back?' that at last he grew enraged, and said: 'I will not be put to these questions. Do you consider, sir, these are the manners of a journalist? Why is England's tail long? Why is Willis's hair bushy?' I attempted to continue the conversation. He was so provoked, that he said: 'Give me no more of this.' He demonstrated an impatience that I should leave, and when I did so, said: 'Do not let us meet tomorrow.'

I left the ground exceedingly uneasy. All the harsh things that had been said about his nature came into my mind. I seemed to myself like a batsman that has faced Malcolm Marshall many times with perfect safety, but at last has had his head knocked off his shoulders. Next morning, I sent him a note, saying that he had the right of it.

Notwithstanding his injunction to me not to call upon him that day, I resolved to go to Old Trafford, where I knew him to be. I entered the press-box there, and perceived that my note had somewhat softened him, and he received me very cordially. Such is the sweetness of nature of the great man, that I found myself unexpectedly at my ease.

Swanton was speaking unfavourably of a certain cricketer who, though regularly selected for England, never yet seemed to score runs on a great occasion. 'He is a great talker on the game, sir, a great talker. Yet no sooner does he take his bat in his hand, than it becomes a tree-trunk to him, and he benumbs all his faculties.' BOSWELL: 'Many would prefer him to Botham, sir.' SWANTON: 'Botham is a vicious man, sir, but very kind to me. If you call a dog Botham, I shall love him.'

Our conversation then turned to the selectors of the England team, and Swanton spoke slightingly of them. BOSWELL: 'Sir, the selectors are patriotic men.' SWANTON: 'Patriotism, sir, is the last refuge of the scoundrel, but it is also the first refuge of the idiot. You may take your choice, sir.' I whispered to him: 'Well, sir, you are now in good humour.' SWANTON: 'Yes, sir, I am.' BOSWELL: 'What, sir, do you consider the prospects of play?' SWANTON: 'Inspissated gloom, sir.'

The Tale of Gatti the Dwarf and Lubo the Elf

J. R. R. TOLKIEN

This is the tale of Gatti the Dwarf and Lubo the Elf, which was told in the Latter Days whenever the hairy-toed race of Journos gathered. It was a tale told with many a merry laugh and many a tankard of goodly ale. It tells also of Bothorn, son of Bothogorn, and of the mighty wizard, Brears the Grey.

It began in the light of a fair morning, when Brears, the Grey Batsman, went out to have colloquy with the Enemy. 'Brears the Grey knows all things,' said Lubo, the golden-haired. 'But my heart likes not his task this morn.'

'Why did he go, then?' piped up Knotty.

'Peace, Halfling,' said Bothorn. 'You speak of what you cannot understand.'

'Bah!' said Gatti, swinging his axe. 'More Elvish magic, I'll warrant. Will we never hear the end of it?'

Lubo was on his feet even as the words left his lips. 'I have not yet heard the Dwarfs speak, save to whinge. Will you and your kind whinge on till the Enemy wins as he likes?'

'I have not heard that the Elves ever did much, save to waft airily outside the off-stump!'

'Peace! And peace again, I say!' said Bothorn. 'The match is between us and the Enemy. Keep your weapons sharp for that encounter.'

'It is well spoken, Bothorn son of Bothogorn,' said Lubo. 'Gatti, good Dwarf, give me your hand. A pledge on it: we shall stand one alongside the other, and fight the Enemy as comrades.'

'Lubo, I accept your hand. None shall say that Dwarf fled while Elf stood fast.'

The door was flung open, and Brears the Grey entered the room. The Company read many things in the face of the wizard. Bothorn, who knew him best, saw a strange light in his deep eyes. 'Speak, Brears,' he said. 'For I would know what your looks betide.'

'I see good, and I see evil,' replied the wizard. 'To start with good tidings: I won the toss.'

'You are a great wizard!' said Gatti.

'Maybe so, good Dwarf, but there was nothing of wizardry in this. Know you not I am sworn to use no magic in the toss? But win I did, and to bat, friends, to bat.'

'But I see grimness in your purposes, O Wise One,' said Lubo. 'And this mislikes me greatly.'

'Ah, how often is it said, you cannot hide jewels from a Dwarf, nor secrets from an Elf?' said Brears. 'But I pray you, leave my secret with me a while.'

'Wise One,' said Lubo. 'I believe the good tidings are for the Free Folk, in their match against the Enemy. The evil tidings are for yourself alone.'

'Pass me my helm, Lubo Gower, my excellent Elf,

and turn your eyes elsewhere. I go to bat. But I must pass on such tidings as I can ere I do so. Marsh Hal, the Balrog, has passed a fitness test this morning and will bowl.'

'But what's a Balrog?' asked little Knotty, who had been keeping quiet and hoping not to be noticed.

'Aye, the little race of Wickies has had little to do with Balrogs,' said Brears. 'But against my will, I fear they shall know more, and that soon. Enough! I go to battle.'

'And I with you!' cried Zap, the mighty man of the forbidden land at the foot of the Dark Continent. 'Newlands!'

With that, Brears and Zap left them, to face the might of this team of Orcs, Goblins and all the worst folk that the Enemy could call on. The light grew very dark, and the learned men of lore consulted their instruments but permitted the battle to start. And in the darkening gloom, the Enemy laid waste before them. One mighty blow felled the giant Zap and a moment later Brears met his nemesis as Marsh Hal, the mighty Balrog, struck.

This left Lubo and Gatti standing alone to defy the Enemy. 'My heart grows faint within me,' said Knotty back in the dressing room. He turned to Bothorn, and asked: 'Can you not go to their aid?'

'Nay, Halfling. Not till the bat that was broken has been mended. That will not be until I do battle on the field of Heading Lee, for thus it is written. It is on the Dwarf and the Elf that our hopes must rest.'

Gatti stood at the crease with his stout legs apart. 'This is more to my liking!' he said. 'My heart rises as battle approaches. A few goodly blows, and I shall feel my blood stir anew.'

'Maybe so, for you are a Dwarf, and Dwarfs are strange folk,' said Lubo. 'But I have my wand, and do not doubt it can do some damage to the Enemy.'

'My axe will do for me. The blade yearns for the taste of leather once again. To battle, Lubo the Elf.'

'To battle, Gatti the Dwarf.'

The Enemy closed in. Gatti raised his axe. 'Enfield! Enfield!' he cried. And he set about him like a man scything corn.

At the other end, Lubo brandished his Elven wand. 'Leicester!' he said. The ball whistled towards him, yet Lubo despatched it with one flick of his slim wrists.

'What magic is this?' called Gatti.

'This is the Elvish way. Do you like it, Master Gatti?'

'Very much,' Gatti replied. 'All that does damage to the Enemy makes my heart sing within me.'

'Then to battle once again, good Friend!'

'To battle, Elf and Friend!'

The sky was utterly dark, and the stillness of the heavy air told of storms. Yet across the pitch the watchers in the dressing room saw the ill-matched pair lay waste before them. Even the Balrog himself was powerless against the Dwarfish axe, and the Elven wand. The balls fell thick as rain among them; but always the Dwarf and the Elf fended them off, or despatched them as they would in the dark tempest of cricket.

The day ended. 'Well, Master Lubo, I have one hundred and twelve,' said Gatti.

'You have passed my count by one,' Lubo replied. 'But I do not grudge it you, so glad am I to have fought alongside.'

'The way you waft your wand ever baffles me, to speak truth,' Gatti said. 'But I would not have it otherwise. I shall not forget this day.'

'Friend Gatti, we have won more than a battle. We have won a friendship. May the Dwarfs and the Elves from henceforth seek conflict against the Enemy alone – never more against each other.'

'It shall be so,' said Gatti. 'Now let us to the victory feast, and ale, cheese, and Branston.'

'Good Gatti, spare me that,' said the Elf. 'But I'll gladly accompany you. We need not share all things. You to your Branston, I'll toast our friendship in the fairy nectar of Bollinger.'

'So be it!' cried Gatti. 'No matter what we sup, victory and friendship are ours for ever.' And ever did it prove thus, as the hairy-toed race of Journos have reported over their ale many a long year since.

The Gnomiad

HOMER

At the first sight of Dawn's red streamers in the East, the noble, much-enduring Gnomius made his way across the alelight pitch. Tears streamed down his cheeks as he made his way into the lofty pavilion. There to meet him was the gallant Zappicus, mighty wielder of the willow bough.

'My Lord Gnomius,' said the stalwart Zappicus. 'I am not a light-headed fool. Yet the mass of men who oppose us today seem to me to spell our doom.'

'My friend,' said Gnomius with subtle intent. 'Bestir yourself and help me pay my devotions to Athene, who has first claim upon me, as she does upon all cricketers.' This was to test Zappicus, who some said had been suborned by Polydux, immortal enemy of the wily Gnomius.

But the loyal Zappicus retorted: 'I have already ordered the slaughter of forty heifers and the delivery of ninety hogsheads of blood-red wine. Thus we shall feast before the match, and make libations to the gods that dwell on high Olympus.'

The wise Gnomius then summoned the entire team around him. 'Noble warriors, let us make our petitions and feast until the beginning of the match. Thus we shall go into battle rejoicing.' The long-haired Essecsonians feasted until the start of play on plentiful meat and sparkling ruddy wine.

The warlike Gnomius then prepared himself for battle, girding himself with strong leg-guards and the sacred helmet, gift of the goddess Athene. Then with Zappicus at his side he went forth across the alelight pitch to meet his foes.

'So you are come again, trouble-loving Gnomius, to pit your wits against our might,' said Gregius, captain of the glory-hunting Surrilonians. 'Then let us to battle, and the gods themselves shall see who carries the day. For you, there will be no return, no welcome home from your joyful wife, no joyous greeting of your happy children. Misery will be your lot this day!'

'Cease your boasting,' retorted the brave Gnomius. 'The gods love deeds, they have no love for prattle.'

Then the Cloud-gatherer sent a mighty bank of black thunder-bringing darkness over the storm-tossed ground, but forebore to send sweet showers. And Polydux, immortal enemy of the much-enduring Gnomius, breathed fear into the hearts of the white-coated wise men who sit in judgement on the play, so that they dare not offer the light to the batting team.

Thus the men of Surrilon went to battle, and hurled blood-red missiles at the long-suffering Gnomius and his partner Zappicus. Soon Zappicus was felled, and man after man followed him, victims of the proud race of fast-bowling Surrilonians. As the slices of fruit-bestudded cake vanish at teatime before a throng of doughty cricketers, so the men of Essecsonia fell

47

before the vengeful bowling of the warriors of Surrilon.

Then out to battle came the fairest player of them all, Pringillius, much beloved of the noble Gnomius. Gnomius went forward to greet him, kissed his forehead, kissed both his lovely eyes, and then his right hand and his left. With tears streaming down his cheeks he said: 'Pringillius, the issue is on the knees of the gods. It is for us to look stern in the face of danger, and see what adventure the immortal gods will send us.'

And then the many-witted Gnomius raised his voice and said: 'Pringillius, the fast bowlers, slingers of mighty missiles, have I am sure, now bowled themselves out, and I am in much fear. For certainly the enemy will now bring on the spin bowlers, and this wicket, sport of the immortal gods, will certainly turn sideways.'

Glory-hunting Gregius overheard him, as was Gnomius' intention. He turned to his wicket-winning fast bowlers, and bade them stand aside. He called the spinners to him and said: 'Tweakers and turners, here is your chance to pit your wits against those of the ever-arrogant Gnomius. For once, he has made a mistake, and has laid himself open to you. Now to your business.'

Bright-eyed Athene, ever the friend of the patient Gnomius, then stepped down from her dwelling on Mount Olympus, and breathed over the pitch, so that not a ball could go off-true. And then she breathed a new fire into the mind of Gnomius, so that he turned to face his new foes with ever-greater courage. She then returned at once to Mount Olympus and beseeched her father, the all-powerful Zeus, to disperse the clouds, harbingers of thunder. When he granted her this boon, the canopy of cloud withdrew, and Guinnessdark shadows stretched out across the alelight pitch.

Gnomius of the nimble wits then returned to battle. With a new light in his eyes and his mighty weapon in his hand, he laid waste about him. The fielders were scattered across the ground like a herd of cattle whom the dancing gadfly has attacked and stampeded. The boundary boards cracked, the hideous groans of despairing men were heard, and the scoreboard ran with runs. Gregius then ran forward, clasped Gnomius around the knees, and burst into an anguished speech. 'I throw myself on your mercy, Gnomius. I did my best to hold these men back from their evil courses.'

But the victory-loving Gnomius looked at him with contempt, and continued to assault the enemy until the sun went down, and the two sides drew apart. The long-haired Essecsonians then gathered around Gnomius. Gnomius of many wiles then ordered the slaughter of five hundred cattle and the broaching of five thousand barrels of blood-red wine, and the baking of several million fruitcakes. They feasted all night, until Dawn had risen from the bed where she sleeps with Lord Tithonius to bring light to the immortals and to men. Thus the second day's play began.

The Love-Song of
J. Derek Pringle

T. S. ELIOT

Let us go then, you and me
When the members are spread out after tea
Like patients etherised upon their various tables.
Let us take a turn around
The littered, half-deserted ground,
Scene of a thousand slipping-ups,
The dropped pork pies and paper cups,
A walk like a tedious innings
That leads to an overwhelming appeal.
Oh! Do not ask how was it.
Let's stay inside our closet.

In the pav the members come and go
Talking of Compton, Hobbs and Co.
And I shall wonder 'do I dare?' and 'do I dare?'
Do I dare to score a century?
Do I dare to eat a cake?
(They will say, his speed has dropped, his action's
    gone.)
I have seen my cricket reputation flicker,
I have seen the eternal pavilion attendant

Refuse to let me in and snicker.
In short I was afraid
And out of form.

Oh, I have been in, been out,
Bowled a spell a thousand times,
I have known the game, have known it all,
I know the batsman's face before his fall.
I have read a thousand times of triumphs and great
    loves.
I have measured out my life with batting gloves.

And would it have been worth it, after all,
Among the pickle and the cups of tea
To have the journos turn, and say to me,
It was my doing, all my own;
To play a game that wakes the members from their
    sleep,
To play and set the universe on end,
To split the heavens with an overwhelming
    appeal?
Instead I've batted, played and missed,
And seen my name, a thousand times,
Get scratched out from the list.

No, I am not Ian Botham, nor was meant to be;
Am a useful man, one that will do
To play nightwatchman, bowl as second change,
Advise the skipper, make up numbers;
Bowl line and length and nudge a run or two,
Careful, politic, professional,
Full of good quotes, but a bit obtuse,

At times, indeed, almost ridiculous.
At times, indeed, almost twelfth man.

I grow old, I grow old,
I shall wear the bottoms of my flannels rolled.

Shall I have highlights dyed into my hair?
Shall I find a ghost and write a book?
I shall wear white flannel trousers and shall walk
    across the pitch,
I have noticed Miss Barbados beckon from a ditch.
I do not think she will beckon to me.
You! Hypocrite spectateur! Mon semblable! Mon
    frère!

Fear and Loathing
at Lord's

A savage journey to the heart of
the Great British Dream

HUNTER S. THOMPSON

We were pulling into St John's Wood Station when
the drugs began to hit.

I remember saying to my leg-man: 'I feel a little
peculiar, is this our stop?' . . . and suddenly we were
wading up to the ankles in weasels, the little bastards
were everywhere, crawling up legs, seeking a pur-
chase, going for the jugular.

A voice was shouting: 'Who turned these bloody
weasels loose?'

'What was that you said?' asked my leg-man, turning towards me. He was wearing a Hawaiian shirt
with a scarlet leather tie, and huge mirror shades.

'Nothing,' I said. 'Let's get off the tube.'

It was nearly eleven and soon play would start at
Lord's. We had a quarter-mile to go, I knew they
would be four hundred extremely tough yards. We
were already completely twisted.

But we were journalists, assigned to attend a Test

match – we had an obligation to COVER THE STORY.

We had been given our expenses in advance, and had spent the lot in a high-speed drug-run through London. My briefcase held a small but serious drug collection: some black nightmare acid, some mescaline, a dozen amyls, assorted uppers and down-ers, a lump of Nepalese hash; also a large bottle of tequila, a dozen limes and a salt shaker full of salt.

We had started early on the acid, cut it with some hash and tequila about ten, cracked a couple of amyls on the tube. Now we had to make it to the Grace Gate and GET IN.

'What was that about weasels?' asked my leg-man. I let it go. The poor bastard would see them soon enough.

'We have to do it,' my leg-man said when we were first asked to go to Lord's. My leg-man is of West Indian extraction, and is six and a half feet tall.

'Right,' I said. 'I tell you, my man, this is the Great British Dream in action. Load up on acid and get down to the cricket.'

Right now the thought of the gateman was bothering me. In no way could we pass as drunk. Strange, menacing vibrations came from us. 'Be calm,' I was telling myself. 'Act normal.'

The man from *The Times* was arguing with the gateman when we arrived. 'Look, there's a ticket for me on the gate, and if it's not here . . .'

Fortunately he didn't recognise me behind my

Peruvian wraparound sunglasses. 'Excuse me butting in, but we're rather late. Our tickets . . .' I waved a couple of tickets in his direction, neither, in fact, valid tickets for the game, for I seemed to have lost our own. The gateman nodded amiably at me, not wanting to inspect what were, in fact, a bus ticket and a bar bill, and continued his conversation with the *Times* man: 'Anybody could come up here and say . . .'

'Didn't I tell you it was easy? We just have to MAINTAIN,' said my leg-man.

'Give me a Mandy and maybe a slug of tequila,' I said. 'I feel I should take the edge off the acid.' Mandies tend to induce a horrible, slobbering, uncoordinated stupor, but that would not make me stand out, not in this crowd. And I needed to fight the frenzy the acid was creating.

'Let's walk around the ground,' my leg-man said. 'We need to get a HANDLE on this story.'

Madness, madness . . . walking through this crowd of purposeful people who eyed us strangely. Lord's has no use for a couple of acidheads. Get a grip. If they nail me here, I'm doomed. A man in a suit and panama hat with a face like a tomato bumped into me. Look out for the bastard weasels! Jesus, did I say that or just think it?

'Where are we?' I asked my leg-man.

'Sponsor's tent,' he replied.

'Can we handle it?' I asked.

'Maybe not. Let's do a couple of mescaline tabs. It'll take the edge off the Mandies.'

'Whatever's right.'

He led me into the tent and sat me at a table. He brought me a large glass of what looked like fruit salad and tasted like alcohol. There was no spoon; in order not to draw attention to myself I ate the fruit with my fingers.

'Jesus, stop doing that,' said my leg-man. 'It's Pimms. Just drink it.'

'Sure . . . Christ, I'm getting a little uneasy.'

'Stay cool. We can maintain.'

All around us, men in suits were milling around, drinking with brutal dedication. 'I don't understand,' I said. 'Aren't we at the cricket?'

'Sure.'

'But no one's watching it.'

'This is a sponsor's tent.'

'It's giving me the fear.'

'Are you kidding? This is close to the heart of the Great British Dream.'

'That's why I'm getting the fear.'

At the next table from me, an orang-utan was burying his noseless face into a drink. I looked up. I was surrounded by orang-utans. They were shouting at each other, and as I looked, a male leant over to a female and started to gnaw at her. I looked down. The carpet beneath us was already stained with blood. 'We're right in the middle of the apehouse,' I whispered.

'Act normal,' said my leg-man. 'Don't run. That's what the bastards WANT us to do.'

Beyond us was a table covered with enough food to feed a small African nation for three months. 'See that?' I said.

'Don't point. If we notice it, they'll put us there and eat us.' I noticed he was crying behind his mirror shades.

'These apes are cannibals too?'

'They don't look on it as cannibalism. It's just like eating dogs and pigs to them.'

'Jesus, we've got to get out.'

With fixed eyes, we walked out, just two refugees from the Love Generation unable to last the pace. With the right kind of eyes, you can stand on top of the Warner Stand and look out towards the Sixties: Kensington Market, Kings Road, the Rainbow . . . Lord's is where the wave broke and rolled back.

The Long Room is where the whole hip world would be every Saturday if the First World War had never taken place. My leg-man and I had walked in while the doorman was explaining to the man from *The Times* that he was not allowed to enter. I could see the religious hush of the place was getting to my leg-man when he genuflected in front of the portrait of W. G. Grace.

The eyes on us were not hostile as they had been back in the sponsor's tent. They were simply wondering. How could a couple of bedrock crazies be strolling through the Long Room? But they knew the way of the world. It was not as if we were women. Since we were here, we clearly had a right to be there. Jesus, what's happening in this world?

We pushed our way through the crowd, and found a place to sit, in front of the pavilion. The acid was wearing off, the Mandies were long gone, but the mescaline was running hot and strong.

We sat awhile and watched some poor victim-geek being bombarded by a band of ferocious black men with some kind of weapon. 'Is THIS the Great British Dream?' I asked.

'It's the Great West Indian Dream,' he said. 'Shut up and pass the tequila and a new lime. Maybe a couple of amyls.'

With the public torturing of the victim-geek continuing all around us, we cracked the amyls and felt that familiar old sledgehammer on the back of the skull. With it came a flash of realisation: the public act of torture and humiliation was what we had come to see. This was the STORY.

No, Lord's is not a good place for psychedelic drugs. Reality itself is too twisted. All around me I could sense that the weasels were closing in.

The Innings of Huckleberry Finn

MARK TWAIN

You don't know about me, without you have read Wisden, but that ain't no matter. That book was made by Mr Graeme Wright, and he told the truth, mainly. Anyway, when it was all through, he called me one of them Wisden Cricketers of the Year, which is a mighty fine thing to be. Folks tell you all manner of wonderful cricketers been Wisden Cricketers of the Year, but I don't know. I don't take no stock in dead people.

Now the way the book winds up is, how in one season I changed from being kind of wild and how the game of cricket has sort of sivilized me. I reckon that's piling it on, maybe. I don't know nothing about sivilizing, because the people at the cricket grounds are so dismal regular and decent I just decide to light out some days. But mostly, as I say, Mr Wright is telling the truth. That season I did learn to be a more considerable cricketer, and some days I felt powerful sivilized. It ain't quite true it happened in one season though. Mostly I reckon it happened in one match, and here's the story of it.

Well, at the beginning of the game, the captain asked if I mind batting number five, and I say, no, I ain't particular. I aim to bat anytime, and go out there and hit the ball middling hard. Three, four, five, it don't signify. A body's got to bat sometime. So the game starts without me, and I got to lying out in the changing room smoking away, and I was powerful lazy and comfortable. Then our batsmen start getting out, so I had to start getting in. It were the waste of a good pipe, but no matter. I druther be batting than smoking at the end of it, so I went out batting.

It warnt like what I expected, though. Those bowlers out there seemed to have something, like it was agin me personal. It got very tiresome and lonesome out there. I felt so lonesome I most wished I was dead. Then comes one ball that near shaved my head, and I reckon it *would* a shaved my head, if I ain't moved it some. Well that ball, it cut one of my breaths in two, and I got only half, and the short half, too.

Batting with me was our captain, but that warnt no good, I could see. Soon as I saw him hopping around and cussing, I knowed that. I would a talked to him and shared some of my troubles, but he had troubles enough all on his own. If he couldn't help his own self, he warnt going to help me, and pretty soon he got out. That's the way it is, I reckon, for the hopping and swearing folk.

Well, then there was nobody out there but me, and all them opposing team, and I got so down-hearted and scared, I wished I had some company. And soon as I wishes it, I saw ole Jim as he clumb out of the pavilion, and comes out on to the field to be my partner. I bet I was right pleased to see him, and right surprised, too, I can tell you. I say: 'Hello, Jim,' and walked down the pitch to talk.

He looked at me kind of wild, and said: 'What's de bowlin' like heah?'

'Never mind the bowling, Jim. What's *you* doing here?' He looked pretty uneasy, and didn't say nothing for a minute. Then he says: 'Dey's reasons. But you wouldn't tell on me ef I uz to tell you, would you, Huck?'

'Blamed if I would, Jim.'

'Well, I b'lieve you, Huck. I done promoted myself to number six. Didn't tell no one. I just run off into the middle, so's I can act like a batsman.'

'What you done this for, Jim?'

'It uz this way. I uz passing by the secretary's office, thinking, well, they got a po reputation, but they awluz treats Jim pooty good. But I noticed there was a Welshman roun these parts lately, en I begin to git a little oneasy. So I git to lis'n at de do', and dat's when I hear things. I niver thought they'd do it, and dat's de truth. They'm gwyne to sell Jim to Glamorgan! Well, I lit out mighty quick, and I git to do some thinking. I heared dat Middlesex is looking for an all-rounder, and dat dey look at me, but dey reckon I never git no chance to bat, so maybe I ain't no all-rounder. So I comes out today, to bat number six, and I reckon if I can git a fifty, they won't send me to Glamorgan, but I kin git by myself to Middlesex as a free cricketer.'

Well, I resolves to help Jim all I could. There was a tolerable long piece of work to be done, but being with Jim, it was better than being lonesome. Besides, work's a funny thing. Sometimes by yourself, work looks most impossible, and like to take up all day, and maybe the next day, too. But when you get to working with some body, and when you get to working *for* some body, and that body is asking your help; well, that effort don't signify. You just get to shoveling that ball away, and the work don't seem like nothing.

I reckon it's the same when you is *being* helped. Leastways, when I starts shoveling the ball, Jim leaves off being so fearful, and *he* starts shoveling the ball. Soon the day was all shoveling and smiting, and the scoreboard just tickering round, like it was doing it all by itself. The runs jist come. It warnt no problem. We jist scored them.

Well, it got to being lunch, and it got to being tea, and it got to being the end of the day, and there was Jim and me. It was a mighty lot of shoveling, I can tell you. Jim and me, we both had centuries, and I most had two. Jim went to Middlesex, to be an all-rounder and a free man and all. I got to being a Wisden Cricketer of the Year, like I says. It was as much Jim's doing as mine, but he ain't complaining, and I guess I ain't neither. But I reckon I got to light out for Australia ahead of the rest. The Test match selectors at Lord's, they'm going to adopt me and sivilize me and I can't stand it. I been there before.

Banksie

VLADIMIR NABOKOV

Banksie, light of my life, flower of the cricket field. My game, my victory, my defeat. Bank-sie: the tongue, bruising itself on a harsh cluster of consonants, is unexpectedly relieved by a lisping Andalusian affirmative: *si*.

She was plain Gill to her team-mates, Gilly in japes at the bar. She was Gillian Banks on the dotted line. She was G. M. Banks in the batting order. She was Gilly-girl standing six-foot-two in one cricket boot. But in my arms she was always Banksie.

Did she have a precursor? Indeed she did, or there might have been no Banksie. A certain fellow boy-child, when I and he were both at prep school. But that sweet bliss of which the angels sing: that I only knew with my Banksie.

As I write these miserable memoirs, the question rises again before me. Was this excessive desire for a member of the England women's cricket team only evidence of a more profound singularity? When I try to analyse my cravings for sporting ladies, my mind is filled with so many electric images of lacrosse players, hockey girls and shot-putters in the maddening complexities of my past, that my reasoning faculties fail me. How little of reason did I ever possess, since first I lay with Banksie!

Now I wish to introduce the following idea. Between the ages of eighteen and twenty-seven, on sporting fields throughout the world, there occur women who, to certain bewitched travellers, reveal their true nature, which is not human. In America, their male equivalents are referred to as 'jocks': these chosen creatures, then, I shall designate 'jockettes'.

Are all sporting ladies jockettes? Of course not. Were this so, we lovers of jockettes, we who suffer from *jockettophila dementia*, would be driven insane long before tea was taken at any match ever played. Nor are good looks the true criterion, any more than is mere size. A jockette will exhibit (but only to few) that bewildering, intoxicating combination of gruffness and acceptance – oh, my Banksie, I can hear you even now as you say to me: 'Well, all right, if you must.' It is not a question of grace, or even power. A jockette is a phenomenon marked by a certainty of purpose: a certain certainty, if you like. An ordinary man, given a team photo, and asked to point out the comeliest, will not necessarily pick out the jockette. You need to be a poet and a lunatic, a scholar and a skulker in shadows, a person of infinite miseries with a phial of hot bubbling poison in your cricket-box. My sweaty, downy darling, you knew, you knew.

The Importance of Being Captain

OSCAR WILDE

THE PERSONS OF THE PLAY

LANE, butler
ALGERNON MONCRIEFF, cricketer
JACK WORTHING, cricketer
THE HON. MISS PHILIPPA SHARPE, selector
LADY PETRONELLA MAY, leader of the selectors

ACT ONE

The players' room at Lord's. LANE *is arranging tea.*
ALGERNON *enters in full batting kit, carrying his helmet*
and gloves.

ALGERNON: I say, Lane, did you see my innings?
LANE: I thought it more polite not to watch, sir.
ALGERNON: That was foolish. I played with great
    feeling. Anyone can play to make runs, but
    sentiment is my forte in batting. I keep
    method for life.
    (*The door opens.* JACK *enters,* LANE *leaves.*)

ALGERNON: My dear Ernest, how surprising to see you.

JACK: Is it so surprising? After all, I have been selected to play for England. I am quite delighted, I must tell you.

ALGERNON: To play for England is merely a bore. Not to play for England is a tragedy. But the match is next week: what brings you to town?

JACK: Oh, pleasure, pleasure. I am to speak with the selectors about becoming captain of England – is that not romantic?

ALGERNON: I call that business. You are to play cricket – that is romantic. But to scheme and negotiate for victory is a mere aspect of commerce. I find captaincy sordid. Besides, captaincy demeans any man who becomes captain, and the job is strangely precarious.

JACK: I remember when Botham was relieved of the captaincy.

ALGERNON: He looks quite twenty years younger now.

JACK: The man himself was quite altered.

ALGERNON: His hair turned quite gold from grief. But tell me, Ernest, what have you been doing? Practising hard in the nets, I have no doubt.

JACK: I never practise. Practice is seen as a kind of virtue, and I have my reputation as a devil-may-care swashbuckler to consider.

ALGERNON: I hope you do not practise in secret, and only pretend to be dilatory. That would be hypocrisy. I was most disappointed by the

lack of evidence for wickedness in your autobiography.

JACK: How do you know about my autobiography?

ALGERNON: My dear fellow, if you will leave manuscripts lying around in dressing rooms, you must expect them to be perused.

JACK: But I needed it today. I had a long journey here by train, and I was sadly in need of something sensational to read.

ALGERNON: I fear there will be trouble over this book.

JACK: Impossible! It is a cricket book pure and simple.

ALGERNON: Cricket is never pure and rarely simple. All of modern sporting journalism depends on that fact. But tell me about your last match. Was it a happy occasion?

JACK: It was happy for my team, and unhappy for the opposition. That is what cricket means. I believe the selectors were impressed by the value of my own innings.

ALGERNON: A selector is a person who knows the score of everyone and the value of no one.
(*The door bursts open and* PHILIPPA *enters.*)

PHILIPPA: Turn your back, Algy, I have something to say to Mr Worthing.

ALGERNON: I cannot allow it.

PHILLIPA: You are too young to be a hypocrite. Wait till you retire and become a journalist. Ernest.

JACK: My darling Philippa, what is it?

PHILIPPA: The leader of the selectors is coming to see you at this very moment, but I feel I must tell you that you can be certain of my vote.

JACK: My own darling!

PHILIPPA: I have long believed that only a man called Ernest can captain England. No other name produces vibrations.

JACK: You would not offer me the job if my name was Jack?

PHILIPPA: But of course not. Now, before the leader arrives, show me how you play the reverse sweep.

JACK: But I —

PHILIPPA: I shall not ask twice, Ernest.

JACK: Then watch, my own sweet Philippa.
(JACK *drops to one knee and mimes the reverse sweep.* LADY MAY *enters.*)

LADY MAY: Mr Worthing! Rise, sir, from this semi-recumbent posture.

JACK: Lady May, I was playing the reverse sweep.

LADY MAY: Pardon me, you are playing nothing of the kind. If you ever play the reverse sweep, be sure I shall be the first to inform you of the fact. Now explain to me the meaning of your presence here at Lord's.

JACK: Lady May, I believe I am to be considered as captain of England.

LADY MAY: On what do you base this claim?

JACK: Did you see my last innings for my county?

LADY MAY: I do not go to county matches.

JACK: Well, my last innings for England then.

LADY MAY: To go to county matches is merely

indiscreet. To attend Test matches is nothing less than vulgar. Do you bet on horses?

JACK: I'm afraid I do.

LADY MAY: I am glad to hear it. I believe all cricketers should have an occupation. What is your record against Malcolm Marshall?

JACK: I was out lbw twice while offering no stroke.

LADY MAY: To be out lbw while padding up once may be regarded as a misfortune. To do so twice looks like carelessness. Now, Mr Worthing, please show me your old school tie, and your Blue.

JACK: I cannot, Lady May.

LADY MAY: And why not?

JACK: I lost them, Lady May.

LADY MAY: And where did you lose them?

JACK: In a cricket-bag.

LADY MAY: A cricket-bag?

JACK: I was travelling to Sydney, and it was sent to Santiago in error. I was flying British Airways.

LADY MAY: The airline is immaterial. Captaincy is quite out of the question, and I would strongly advise you find a school or a good university before the cricket season is quite over. Come, Philippa.

(LADY MAY *sweeps out in majestic indignation, followed by* PHILIPPA.)

JACK: This is frightful.

(ALGERNON *is laughing immoderately*.)

JACK: This is no laughing matter.

ALGERNON: There is only one thing worse than being England captain, and that is not being England captain.

JACK: Cricketers never talk anything but nonsense.

ALGERNON: Nobody ever does.

(*Curtain*.)

Imran Khan

SAMUEL TAYLOR COLERIDGE

In St John's Wood* did Thomas Lord
A stately pleasure–dome decree:
Where deep the sacred tube–line roared
Through caverns desolate and broad –
By name the Jubilee!
So twice five furlongs fertile ground
With sponsors' tents was girdled round:
And there were pitches bright with sinuous rills†
Where flourished many a linseed–scented bat,
And watched by members ancient as the hills,
Roused from their slumbers at the cry: 'How's
    that!'
But oh! that deep romantic place was set
And circled by a world of dolour!
A savage place! As full of care, disease and debt
As e'er a losing match had been beset
By a captain wailing for his demon bowler!

---

* This is, of course, pronounced 'Sinjun's Wood'.
† A rill is a kind of late cut, played very close to the
stumps.

To flee the world the people still came flocking
Frighted by the horror and the mocking,
Knowing once inside all spite and strife would
   fade,
Once through the gate, all woe would be mislaid,
That in this pleasant place, you never saw
Ancestral newsmen prophesying war.
An endless queue with but a single notion
Five miles meandering with a mazy motion.
A batsman scored a century
In a vision once I saw,
An innings delicate and grand,
Part of a second-wicket stand
And oh! 'Twas grand to see.
Could I revive within me
His strokeplay and his skill,
To such a deep delight 'twould win me
That I, when I had drunk my fill
Might build that dome in air!
That sunny dome! The drinks! The ice!
Such glorious days as I've spent there!
And all shall cry, How's that! How's that!
His floating eyes, his flashing bat!
Weave a circle round him thrice
And close your sporting eyes with dread,
For he on sandwiches has fed
And drunk the tea of paradise.

Note:

This poem was written after the author had fallen into a reverie. He had consumed several large ones before lunch. On waking he wrote the above lines. His train of thought was then broken by a passing Somerset player (one who had played for a small village side in Devon, Porlock CC). On this inter-ruption, the vision was shattered into fragments, never to be reconstituted.

Waiting For Grace

SAMUEL BECKETT

The top of the Warner Stand, Lord's. SMYTHE *looks out through binoculars. He lowers them, shakes them, puts them at his eyes again. Enter* BROWNE.

SMYTHE: Nothing to be done.
BROWNE: So they say, so they say. And yet I've
    been to all the first-class grounds.
SMYTHE: And?
BROWNE: And what?
SMYTHE: You've been to all the first-class grounds.
BROWNE: Certainly I have.
SMYTHE: And will go again.
BROWNE: That I don't know.
SMYTHE: What do you mean, you don't know?
BROWNE: Who knows anything?
SMYTHE: Nothing, then.
    (SMYTHE *raises the binoculars again, lowers them,*
    sighs.)
BROWEN: What do you see?
SMYTHE: Nothing.
BROWNE: What about the cricket?
SMYTHE: Oh, the cricket.
BROWNE: Can you see the cricket?

SMYTHE: (*Furiously*) Of course I can see the bloody cricket!

BROWNE: (*Hurt, stiffly*) I think I shall leave you now.

SMYTHE: Go, then.

BROWNE: Right. Goodbye.

SMYTHE: Goodbye.

(BROWNE *does not move.*)

BROWNE: I'll leave as soon as he gets here, then.

SMYTHE: Who?

BROWNE: Who what?

SMYTHE: What are you talking about? Illuminate me.

BROWNE: You are leaving. Telling me what you are waiting for.

SMYTHE: Or who.

BROWNE: Or who.

(*Pause.* SMYTHE *raises his binoculars half-heartedly, lowers them.*)

This was the spot.

SMYTHE: This was the spot. At the top of the Warner Stand, he said, towards the left.

BROWNE: So this is where we are waiting for Grace.

SMYTHE: He said he might be late.

BROWNE: He is late.

SMYTHE: If he said Wednesday.

BROWNE: If he said Wednesday and meant this Wednesday, this very Wednesday.

SMYTHE: He said to wait.

BROWNE: We waited yesterday.

SMYTHE: Yesterday was not Wednesday.

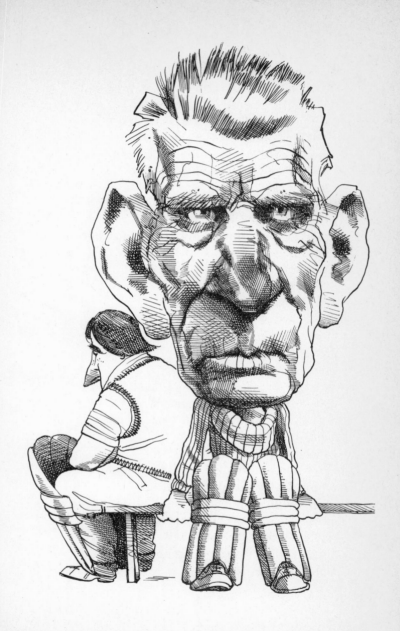

BROWNE: Wasn't it?

SMYTHE: I don't know.

BROWNE: It's the right stand.

SMYTHE: If he said the Warner Stand.

BROWNE: (*Furiously*) Nothing is certain when you're about.

SMYTHE: Calm, calm . . . you know the story about Denis Compton's new bat?

BROWNE: Yes.

SMYTHE: Tell it to me.

BROWNE: Be quiet!

SMYTHE: Denis Compton, on arriving at Lord's and finding himself without a bat . . . go on.

BROWNE: Be quiet, I said!

(*Silence.*)

SMYTHE: That was four.

BROWNE: What was?

SMYTHE: Aren't you watching the cricket?

BROWNE: I suppose so.

SMYTHE: Borrow my binoculars.

(BROWNE *sighs.*)

I said, borrow my binoculars.

(BROWNE *takes the binoculars, and peers all round him.*)

BROWNE: I can't see him.

SMYTHE: Do you think he will be here after tea?

BROWNE: We could come back tomorrow. The game will be going on still.

SMYTHE: There is no point in staying here.

BROWNE: Besides, the light will go soon.

SMYTHE: Did he say anything about the light?

BROWNE: Of course not.

SMYTHE: But he did say he'd come?

BROWNE: He said something.

SMYTHE: I think we've had the best of the day's play.

BROWNE: Let's go, then.

SMYTHE: Yes, let's go.

(*They do not move.*)

The Leg-Spinner

HAROLD PINTER

ACT ONE

Pause.
ANSON *and* DAVIES *are standing in the slips. They assume a crouch position.*
Pause.
A ball is bowled.
They leave their crouch positions. Silence for thirty seconds.

ANSON: Blocked it again.

DAVIES: I could do with a nice catch. I haven't had a nice catch – I don't know – I haven't had a nice catch since I can't tell you when.

ANSON: Haven't you?

DAVIES: No.

ANSON: Oh.

DAVIES: It's hard to keep a place in a team these days.

(*Pause. A ball is bowled.*)

I mean, look at it. They give all the places away to them nigs, don't they? Nigs and South Africans and Rhodesians. Indians, Pakis, Aussies, Kiwis. Even bloody Danes. They'd

sooner have nigs these days. They all would.
What's an old pro like me supposed to do? I'm
clean as they come. Fit as a flea. I'm fit as a
flea, I keep myself up. That's the secret of it,
you see.

(*Pause. A ball is bowled.*)

ANSON: I can see that.

DAVIES: Ah! If I could only get down to Sidcup
Cricket Club.

ANSON: Sidcup Cricket Club?

DAVIES: Left my blasted bloody cricket boots in
the changing room there. I was there for a
benefit match, and I had so much to do I left
my boots there. Best pair of boots ever made,
they were. Made to my foot. Like a second
skin. I am surprised I can play cricket at all
without them. These modern things, they
aren't no bloody good. Look at them.
Rubbish. You see, they've lost the boot-
maker's art.

(*Pause. A ball is bowled.*)

I went to the secretary and said, could I have
the Sunday League match off, so I can get
down to Sidcup Cricket Club to get my
blasted bloody boots. Do you know what he
said to me?

ANDON: No.

DAVIES: Piss off, he said!

ANSON: Did he?

DAVIES: Piss off! I got my rights, I told him, I'm
an old pro, no one's got more rights than me.

(*Pause. A ball is bowled.*)

83

ANSON: I ordered a slice of Dundee cake yesterday.
In the tea-room. It came on a cardboard plate.
I couldn't eat it. I only like Dundee cake on a
china plate.

DAVIES: That secretary, he only likes nigs.

ANSON: I was sitting there, just drinking my tea,
not eating the cake. And the tea lady came to
me, and she said, quite suddenly, would you
like my body?

DAVIES: I've had 'em say the same to me.

(*Pause. A ball is bowled. The ball flies off an edge
and passes between* ANSON *and* DAVIES. *Enter*
MICK.)

MICK: What's the game?

(*Curtain.*)

ACT TWO

The opposite end, a few seconds later. MICK *and*
DAVIES *are standing in the slips.*

MICK: Did you see it?

DAVIES: I —

MICK: Are you seeing the ball well? Are you seeing
it like a football? Are you seeing it like a
breadfruit?

DAVIES: No, I —

MICK: You remind me of a bloke who used to play
for Hampshire. Built like you, a little fairer.
He started to miss catches. Well, we had to let
him go, didn't we? That was the only morally

84

defensible position. Gave him the bullet, gave
him the push. The old heave-ho.
(*Pause. A ball is bowled.*)
Perhaps you are considering a move into
coaching.

DAVIES: I —

MICK: But do you have the qualifications? Have
you read all the right books? Do you
understand the importance of the initial
movement of the back foot, the need to make
the back-lift an integral part of the stroke, the
correct position of the left elbow relative to the
left shoulder, the need at all times to
remember that cricket is a sideways game?
(*Pause. A ball is bowled.*)
But perhaps you don't care. Perhaps you just
go out and hit the ball any old how. Perhaps
you play by the sweet light of nature. Perhaps
you are an entirely instinctive player, with
reactions of quicksilver. And your failure to
catch that ball was an aberration, a chance in a
million, a next to impossible occurrence. Is
that what you are telling me?

DAVIES: I got my rights.

MICK: Are you a foreigner?

DAVIES: Born and bred in the British Isles!
(*Pause. A ball is bowled.*)

MICK: Because you remind me of a foreigner who
used to bowl a bit of leg-spin. He had all the
tricks, and a few more besides. Obviously he
bowled the leg-spinner, the one that moves
away from the right-hander. That's obvious.

85

He also bowled the flipper, that goes straight on and accelerates off the pitch, thereby deceiving the batsman by its lack of lateral movement and its rapid, skidding bounce. He bowled another straight one that appeared to dig in and bounce higher than expected, one designed to catch the batsman in two minds, and a third variety of straight delivery that was perfectly innocuous, but further sowed the seed of doubt in the striker's mind. Naturally he had a googly. You wouldn't expect him not to have a googly, would you? In fact, the very genius of the man was shown in the googly, or rather, in the fact that he had not one but two different kinds of googly. The googly being the ball that moves in towards the right-hander, the wrong'un, as every schoolboy knows. He had one googly that was possible to pick, so that the batsman would feel himself master of the situation. He would be lulled into a false sense of security, only to be undone by the second googly, which was so well disguised it was never picked at all by any batsman. It was all a matter of the flexibility of the wrist and the strength in the fingers, allied to an indomitable mental strength.

(*Pause. A ball is bowled.*)

So you are ready to bowl, I suppose.

DAVIES: You just try it, mate!

MICK: Come again?

DAVIES: You just try it, mate. You just try it. (*He raises his fists.*) I've used these, used 'em before.

You mess with an old pro, you see what you get.

(*Long pause. A ball is bowled.*)

MICK: So you'd like to bowl the next over, would you? Well, that's just dandy.

DAVIES: Not me, mate. You've got the wrong bloke.

MICK: I can't have done. You're the only bloke I've spoken to about the next over. I need a leg-spinner. And you are the answer to my dreams. The man to fulfil my deepest wishes. What do you think you are, if you don't bowl leg-spin? What do you mean by coming here and telling me you don't bowl leg-spin? Just tell me what exactly it is that you mean.

(*Pause. A ball is bowled. It flies off an edge and passes between* MICK *and* DAVIES.)

DAVIES: Look . . . if you want me to go, I'll go . . . but if you'd just let me . . . just let me get down to Sidcup Cricket Club and get my . . . get down to . . .

(*Long pause.*)

(*Curtain.*)

The Oval Diaries

29 August–3 September 1985

SAMUEL PEPYS

---

29. I up early, it being the first day of the Sixth Test match, at the Oval, and bidden to attend. This is, to watch from an executive box the five days, where my Lord hopes I will do much business with the company. Dressed in a silk suit, which cost me much money, and a fine cloak with gold buttons. To the Dog for my morning draught, where the talk is all of cricket. Some say that England, leading the series 2 to 1, will surely win the Ashes; others taking the opposite part foresee an Australian victory. Then by land to the Oval, where I did break my fast with a brave dish of neat's tongue. I did make game with the waitress, a good handsome wench, and talked much of business with the company. At times did watch the cricket, at which I marvelled greatly. Felt much for Mr Tthy. Robinson, who did sorely miss out. Mr Dvd. Gower and Mr Gr. Gooch batted with much freedom. Together, they scored 351 for the second wicket. Methinks the Ashes are settled and the battle as good as won. Did drink a pint or two of wine in the final

session, and was a little too free to make mirth with Mr Thos. Clarke, he being a sober and an upright man. After play to the Leg, where much discussion of merits of this England side, against that of 1953. Great talk of our chances in the winter against the West Indies, which I believe will come to nothing. Home, and so to bed.

30. Up betimes, and to the office, where infinite of business. Was resolved to reach the ground by lunch, which I did, but fear I had left some work undone. At the executive box, did find a great lunch ready: viz. a dish of marrow bones. A leg of Mutton. A loin of veal. A dish of fowl, three pullets and two dozen larks, all in a dish. A great Tart. A dish of anchovies. A dish of prawn and cheese. The company was of men of much influence, but they did not look greatly at the cricket. I was not a little impatient of this, it being a day of much splendour. The Australian team, much cried up when they arrived in the spring, did look in great disarray, and surely cannot but lose both match and Ashes. Mr Gooch did miss his double century by 4 runs. England lost their last nine wickets for 91, which was something disappointing after yesterday, but the Australians batted worse than did seem possible, and were 145 at close. Cannot see that they will avoid the follow-on. I was exceeding free in dallying with the serving wench, and she not unfree to take it. Then home where did work on my accounts, and find I am worth 500*l* more than I had thought, at which my heart was glad and blessed God.

31. All of the morning at home, lying abed with my wife, then to the Oval for the cricket. It being Saturday, there was less talk of business in the executive box, and the company very merry. Did drink several pints of wine before lunch, which was the best venison pasty that ever I had in my life. Borrowed a perspective glass belonging to one of the company, and did marvel to see the faces pulled by Mr Php. Edmonds at bowl. England in command all day. Australia forced to bat on, at which some of my fellows did criticise, saying the Australians had by this their only chance of saving the series. I did speak up loud for Mr Gower, and praised him for taking the bolder course. At day's end, Australia needed a full 161 runs to save defeat by an innings, which does show both Gower and I have the right of it. Made much game of this in the company, and did drink several pints of wine after the play was done. Then to the Cock, where much more drinking and talk. Thence home, and much troubled in finding the way thereto.

1. Lord's day. Exceeding ill all day. Did suspect I had taken food poisoning at the venison pasty that I ate yesterday. To the parish church for sermon, which was very tedious, and during it, God forgive me, I slept. Very ill all day. Did think to send for the doctor, but methinks doctors often prove more trouble than their worth. Great hopes of seeing the victory tomorrow. To bed.

2. Up betimes, and rose today without any pain,

which makes me think that my pain yesterday was nothing but my drinking too much the day before. Straight to my office, where did work in much haste, so to be at the cricket by start of play, believing that play would not last long that day, England being so mighty. Arrived at eleven, and no one but myself in the executive box. The waitress came to ask what I required. I was very bold with her, and, we being alone, soon discovered that, in the Latin, *nulla puella negat*. Australia did succumb to England, making but 129 for all their wickets, at which England won the Ashes 3 to 1. Mr Ls. Taylor took the final wicket. Did wonder much at the change come over Mr Botham, so fine has his cricket been this summer. He has taken 31 wickets in all, at which only he seems unsurprised. He did sometimes bowl with a pace like that of a West Indian. Mr Gower was exceeding merry on the balcony after the match, and told Mr Ptr. West: 'I'll warrant the West Indians be quaking in their boots.' Later met with Mr Math. Engel, the scribe, who told me that Gower's batting this summer does represent the greatest comeback in history since that of Charles II, at which I cannot disagree. We played a while at ninepens, at which I lost 5s. So back home by land, and after supper, to bed.

The Case of the Masked Captain

ARTHUR
CONAN DOYLE

I

To Sherlock Holmes, she was always *the* barmaid. I have never heard him mention her in any other way. It was not that he felt any tenderness for her, for all emotions were abhorrent to his cold and precise mind. And yet there was but one woman to him, and that was Maureen Jones, barmaid of the Highwayman, Nottingham, of dubious and questionable memory.

I returned to our lodgings at Baker Street quite early one summer evening to find Holmes pacing the room swiftly, eagerly, with his head sunk on his chest. I knew this mood of old. He would ever alternate between cocaine and ambition; on this occasion he had commenced a new case, and had cast aside his drug-created dreams.

'Ah, Watson,' he cried as I entered. 'I have

something here that may interest you – even after you have, as I perceive, spent the day at the cricket.'

'Who said so?'

'My dear Watson I need no one to tell me so. You are wearing your panama, and you only ever wear it on sporting occasions. There is an air of well-being and content about you that seldom attends you after you have been to the races. And lastly there is a splash of mud on the left leg of your trousers, of that peculiar yellow tinge that in London is only found in St John's Wood.'

I could not help laughing at this. 'Indeed, I have been watching the Australian touring side play Middlesex at Lord's. How ridiculously simple you always make it sound,' I said. 'And yet I know I could never do as much myself.'

'Precisely. You see, but you do not observe. But come, Watson, what do you make of this?'

He passed me a note, which bore neither date nor signature nor address.

'At seven this evening', it said, 'a gentleman will call on you. He desires to consult you on a very delicate matter that is of the deepest importance to the most important body in England. Be in your chamber at this hour, and do not take it amiss if your visitor wears a mask.'

'This is indeed a mystery,' I remarked. 'What do you imagine it is all about?'

'I have no data yet, Watson. It is a capital mistake to theorise without data. But listen! If I mistake not, our client approaches.'

A powerful, heavy step was heard on the stairs, and the door was given a firm, assertive knock.

'Come in!' said Holmes.

The man who entered could hardly have been more than five foot eight inches in height, yet he seemed to fill our little room, so regal was his bearing. He had the chest and the limbs of a Hercules. Immense power and physical well-being flowed from him. From his face, he appeared to be a man of strong character, with a broad, strong chin capped with a small, carefully trimmed beard. He was dressed in cricket clothes, and wore a black vizard mask.

'You have my note?' he asked, in a curiously high, yet authoritative voice.

'Pray take a seat,' said Holmes. 'This is my friend and colleague, Doctor Watson, who is my indispensable assistant. Whom have I the honour of addressing?'

'You may call me Baron von Gatt. It will suffice. Please excuse this mask; the august and important person for whom I act as agent wishes the strongest possible secrecy to be wrapped around this matter.'

'I see.'

'The case revolves around the England cricket team, and implicates no less a person than the captain.'

'I am aware of that,' Holmes said. 'Please take a seat, Prince Michael. You shall not lose your throne in Enfield because of my indiscretion, nor your captaincy of the England cricket team.'

With a cry, the man flung his mask to the floor. 'I am Prince Michael,' he said. 'Why should I deny it?'

'Why indeed?' said Holmes. 'Pray explain your case, Your Majesty.'

'You have heard of Maureen Jones?'

'Kindly look her up in my index, Doctor.' I rose, and consulted Holmes's massive filing system, finding Jones sandwiched between Jessop and Kallicharan. 'Hum! Principal singer at La Scala. Played for the England women's cricket on seventeen occasions, averaging fifty-two. Retired after purchasing a hostelry called the Highwayman in Nottingham. Both activities used to further her career as an adventuress. Quite so. I take it Your Majesty has become entangled with her.'

'Precisely so. I —'

'Was there a secret marriage?'

'No. There is a letter I wrote —'

'Forgery.'

'And a photograph taken of the two of us in the garden.'

'Your Majesty has committed an indiscretion.'

'I was mad. Insane.'

'And Maureen Jones?'

'Threatens to send the photograph to Lord's. As you know, an unblemished life is of vital importance to the captain of the England cricket team. Also she will send the photograph to my fiancée, Countess Piotrina von der May, who is herself a pillar of respectability, as well as obsessively jealous. She will not hesitate to break off the engagement. This would seriously threaten my position on the throne of Enfield.'

'Leave this with me, Your Majesty. I trust I shall

have good news for you soon, after I have had time to think this little matter over.'

II

The aroma of shag tobacco was heavy in the air when I arose the following morning. It was clear that Holmes, as was his habit when engrossed in a case, had not been to bed, but had sat awake pondering the matter and smoking. He showed not the slightest sign of fatigue: his eyes shone keenly, and he sprang from his chair as I entered.

'Watson!' he said. 'Can I count on you for assistance?'

'Assuredly.'

'You do not mind breaking the law?'

'Not in the least.'

'Then put your revolver in your pocket and catch an evening train to Nottingham. Take a cab to the Highwayman, and when there, follow these instructions to the letter.' He proceeded to explain the steps I must take. 'I can rely on you, Watson?'

'Absolutely.'

'Good old Watson. Come, the game's afoot, and Miss Maureen Jones is in for an evening that may surprise her.'

Thus it was that I set out with Holmes's instructions in my head, my old service revolver in my pocket, and the thrill of adventure in my heart. I arrived at the pub at precisely the time Holmes requested.

The Highwayman was a large, prosperous place set in its own grounds. It was clearly well run and popular: a further testament to the energies and abilities of Maureen Jones. I went straight to the bar, which was magnificently appointed, dominated by french windows that opened into the beautifully tended grounds. There was Miss Jones herself, serving drinks. She was a woman of superb figure, and a cast to her features that, in another, I would have called nothing less than queenly. She was conversing with a disreputable old toper by the bar, a man with a florid complexion, blazer, and MCC tie. He was talking disconnectedly about Barrington's Test match average. She left him, and asked what I would like in tones of singular mellowness and sweetness.

Having ordered my refreshment, I sat at the bar for exactly ten minutes, as Holmes had instructed. I wondered where he had secreted himself. Then, the ten minutes being passed, I walked purposefully from the bar. I returned precisely one minute later to speak the words Holmes had given me.

'My God!' I said. 'The Australian touring party has just pulled up outside in a coach!'

At once there was pandemonium. The customers in the bar left their drinks unfinished and scattered, save for the florid gentlemen at the bar. Miss Jones herself ran to one end of the bar, stooped, and then promptly stood again. 'Come, Watson,' said the florid drinker. 'It is time to make our departure.'

'Holmes!' I gasped. I would never have recognised him had he not spoken. With his disguise he had altered his entire demeanour. His very soul seemed to vary with every part he assumed. Grasping my arm, he escorted me out into the open.

'Well, Watson,' he remarked. 'I think I have it.'

'The photograph?'

'At any rate, I know where to lay hands on it.'

'How?'

'She showed me.'

'I am still in the dark.'

'Let me explain,' he said, laughing greatly. 'When a woman feels herself in great danger, she will invariably run to whatever she treasures most. In her opera days, Miss Jones would have made for her music case. When a cricketer, it would have been her bat. Now, it was to the photograph. It is behind a secret panel, which is itself behind the bar. At six tomorrow morning, we shall walk in with friend Prince Michael, and remove it.'

'Amazing, Holmes!'

'A trifle, Watson. All women, even the finest of them, are very predictable creatures.'

III

With dawn just broken, Holmes led the Prince and myself to the french windows that led to the bar, and quietly levered them open. He stepped behind the bar. 'It will be here, Your Majesty.'

'I am all impatience.'

'Which shall shortly be satisfied.'

Holmes leant down, and within a short while, there was a gratifying click. He stood up with a large

photograph, and a letter. He placed these on the bar:
the picture showed Miss Jones alone, in a revealing
pose that was startling in its power and beauty. The
letter was addressed, 'Sherlock Holmes Esq. To be
left until called for'. My friend tore it open. It read:

My dear Mr Sherlock Holmes,
You really did it very well. You took me in
completely. It was not until after the alarm about
the Australian cricketers had died down, that I
realised how completely you had made me
betray myself. But I fear you have taken on an
assignment in vain.

I love another and better man than Prince
Michael. Last night, I ran to his side, and by the
time you read this I will be married to Lord
David, Duke of Leicestershire, he of the golden
curls, the man who should rightly be captain of
England. Prince Michael can do what he may
without hindrance from a woman he has cruelly
wronged. I leave a photograph he may care to
possess, and I remain, Mr Sherlock Holmes,
very truly yours in sport,
Maureen Gower *née* Jones

'What a woman! What a woman!' said Prince
Michael. 'If only she had been of my class, what a
princess she would have made!'
'Indeed, it would seem the lady is of a very different class from yourself,' said Holmes. 'I fear I have
failed you, Your Majesty.'
'Not at all!' cried the Prince. 'Her word is

inviolate. If she says I am safe, then I am so! How can I reward you – my best bat? My England blazer ?'

'Your Majesty has something I would value even more highly.'

'Name it!'

'That photograph.'

The Prince looked on him in amazement. 'Maureen's photograph? Take it, if you wish.'

'Thank you, Your Majesty. And now I have the honour to wish you a very good morning.'

And that was how a scandal that threatened to overwhelm English cricket and the little princedom of Enfield was averted, and how the best-laid plans of Sherlock Holmes were beaten by a woman's wit. And when he speaks of Maureen Jones, or of her photograph, it is always under the honourable title of *the* barmaid.

Under St John's Wood

DYLAN THOMAS

FIRST VOICE: It is summer, a pale yellow lemony
blackshadowed moonlit night, night in a small
village that has moved – but only for a while –
into the big inkblack city. The village is
gathered around a few acres of bright green,
light green, fielder-crisscrossed grass,
surrounded by stands empty as old maids and
hopeful as young ones. And all of the people
of this shifting, silent village are sleeping now.
Hush, the cricketers are sleeping, the writers, the
commentators, the wives, the forgiving, eye-
wandering fellow-travellers. Young girls glide
in their dreams to secret trysts behind the
pavilions of nowhere. Cricketers sleep,
pursued by glory and horror, beer and bawdy,
snoring as they read the headlines of their
dreams.
You can hear the dew falling on the outfield, you
can hear the pindropping, breathstopping hush
deep in the night of the day before the Test
match begins.
Listen. It is night, silently winding through St
John's Wood. Listen. The village is dreaming

in its temporary home, the Llamedos Hotel.
From where you are, you can hear their
dreams. Brian Cat, fifty years on radio, dreams
of . . .

SECOND VOICE: . . . never such match as ever he
commented on, in the leather-smiting, willow-
wielding, stump-scattering tapes of his crickety
past, for as the game unfolds before him, the
long-dead cricketers come slithering and
sidling up to him.

FIRST DEAD: Remember me, Brian?

BRIAN CAT: You're Slogger Williams!

FIRST DEAD: I got caught out in Taunton.

SECOND DEAD: Do you see me, Brian? I'm
Johnnie Jarvis, what you said was one of the
characters of the game. I came to a bad end.
Very enjoyable.

FIRST DEAD: How is it above?

SECOND DEAD: Is there sun and onions?

FIRST DEAD: Beer and wickets?

SECOND DEAD: Clapping for sixes?

FIRST DEAD: Cake and sandwiches?

SECOND DEAD: Young girls in dresses?

FIRST DEAD: Bosoms and googlies?

SECOND DEAD: Do they still pass the hat round?

FIRST DEAD: What's the smell of cut grass?

BRIAN CAT: Oh my dead dears!

FIRST VOICE: From where you are, you can hear
along the hotel corridors and inside the
sleeping rooms, where Jones the Hook dreams
of . . .

JONES: . . . Runs and runs and runs. Cover drives

and leg glances. The long straight hit that reaches the Nursery.

SECOND VOICE: And doffing his cap to the applauding walls of his silent bedroom, he turns in his sleep where his bat lies tucked in beside him.

JONES: There'll be more runs to get tomorrow.

FIRST VOICE: Along the corridor sleeps Thomas Trundle, first change bowler, played ten Tests and coming up to thirty, counting his money in his sleep.

THOMAS TRUNDLE: In my benefit year I shall have a company six-a-side tournament every weekend, and company dinners every day. I shall sell my England blazer for two hundred pounds.

SECOND VOICE: Snoring across the same room, Dancing Rees, the wicket keeper . . .

DANCING REES: . . . catches a ball and eats it . . .

FIRST VOICE: . . . while across the corridor Nogood Boyo the all-rounder is . . .

NOGOOD BOYO: . . . up to no good.

SECOND VOICE: Captain Lewis, respectable even in his dreams, lies in bed in his blazer with his tie knotted tight to his chin.

CAPTAIN LEWIS: I'm so nice and good and kind I'm certain to be on television.

FIRST VOICE: While Curly Bevan, batsman and one-time captain, lies back and dreams of . . .

CURLY BEVAN: . . . Bollinger.

FIRST VOICE: While Owen the Manager exhorts him to greater efforts.

OWEN THE MANAGER: Put your back into it, Curly! Let's see you drink! I want another magnum down you before lunch. Who's in charge here, by God?

SECOND VOICE: Nogood Boyo stirs in his sleep, but does not rouse Lily Smalls, sleeping like a wicked dormouse beside him.

LILY SMALLS: He doesn't get maidens any more, but he's still trying.

FIRST VOICE: Nogood Boyo . . .

NOGOOD BOYO: . . . riding a whisky bottle, hunts naked women through the woods of the night . . .

SECOND VOICE: . . . and says . . .

NOGOOD BOYO: . . . I want to be Good Boyo, but they won't let me.

FIRST VOICE: Time passes. The Llamedos Hotel stirs in its sleep and disturbs its blankets. Dawn raises an eyebrow over the horizon. Night prepares to withdraw gracefully, and to take its dreams as it goes. The principality of the sky grows lighter, and the sun stretches its legs and prepares to shine over another Test match day.

Prologue to the Teste Matche Tales

GEOFFREY CHAUCER

Whan that Aprille with his sonne brighte
The chille of March hath halfway put to flighte,
And folken in their gardens start to swinke
And poshen folken Pimmies start to drink,
The dayseyes in the outfield gan to flowre
And groundsmen lepe astride the rattlinge mowre,
So grass is short and daies growe evre longe
And tea-ladyes all bursten into songe,
Thanne longen folke to go and watch crickette
And see the batter cope with greene wickette.

Bifel thatte in this seson on a day
In London at the Tavern as I lay
Redy to wenden to a cricket match
The second Teste I was all set to watch.
But natheless whil I have time and space
Er firther in my match report I pace
And er I tell yow of the three one-dayeres
I first shal something tell of all our playeres.

The captaine first, and he a worthye man,
That fro the time that he first bigan
To play the game, he lovede tactics,
Leadership, psychologie, and tricks.
A docotore of philosophie, this fellowe,
And when at batte he hummede of the cello.
His haire beneathe his helmette al was greye
But he could lede the yonge folke al day.
He had taken many a soverein pris
And thoghe thatte he was worthy, he was wis.
He was not talle, like a church's steeple,
But this man had a degree in peple.

A battere ther was, a wontoun and a jollye,
But sometimes given o'er to fits of follye.
He mighte scor an hundred runnes full quicke
Or get out flashing by the offe-sticke.
To play defensively he had no luste,
Alway with him twas shitte or buste.
He had a hede right full of golden curles
And knewe the way to talke to pretty girles.
Scoring runs he found a thing quite fine
Yet seemede to preferre drinkinge win.
Of gritte and effort he did seem to lacke
And of his nature he was ful laid-backe.

We had with us was an al-roundere,
A mightye manne, a bit of a boundere,
He scorede much wherever cricket playede,
Not only ronnes, or so the paperes sayde.
He coulde muchel of wanderinge by the weye
Long-haired he was and playede at cardes al day.

Long yeres ago, his mighty deeds wer done,
And always playede the game as if for fun.
His crickette left he pretty much to chaunce,
He could of love the old daunce.

We had with us a fast bowllere,
Whose port was alway ful of sad doloure,
His deeds had made the crickette world amazede
With whirling arms and with his eyes all glazede,
His run-up was a windmil prance
He semeth like a man caughte in a trance.

A spinnere too we had, a sorry knave
Who knew not how our cricketteres behave,
A left-handere few batsmen knew to matche
And for a sponsor he would weare a Swatche.
He loved rancour, enmity and feud,
And alway to his captaine he was rude.
He had a tricky bitche for a wife*
And chose a mightye man to write his life.

And thus we gan to riden on our weye
To see the cricket for the next five day.

---

* This line contributed by my old friend Frances Edmonds.
S. B.

EDITOR'S NOTES

TRANSLATION:
This will be of particular use for those who are
studying the above text for A level. Editorial com-
ments appear in italics.

When the clement weather of April has more or less
disposed of the unpleasantness of March, and people
start to work in their gardens while the upper classes
knock back glasses of Pimms, and daisies start to
appear in the outfield and groundsmen spend a lot of
time with the mower, when the grass is short and the
days get longer, and tea-ladies start singing, then
people have a great desire to go and watch cricket, and
watch batsmen struggling on a bright green snakepit.

It was at this time of year, as it happens, that I
happened to be lying [*perhaps on the floor, but this is not
certain*] at the Tavern, getting ready to go to a cricket
match, the second Test, if you want the details. But
never mind all that; while I have a moment before I
start my match-report and the recap about the Texaco
Trophy, I had better tell you something about the
players.

I shall start with the captain, a very worthy man. From
the time that he first started to play the game, he loved
tactics, leadership, applied psychology, and ingenious
ploys. He was a Doctor of Philosophy, this person,

and liked to hum a certain 'cello solo [*one of the Razamovsky quartets, as a matter of fact*] while he was batting. His hair underneath his helmet was completely grey, but he was perfectly capable of leading the young players. He had won all kinds of things, and he was not only frightfully nice, he was frightfully clever as well. He was not enormous, but he had a degree in people.

There was a batsman, a pleasant if somewhat careless chap, whose brain would sometimes fly out of the window. He could score a ton in about ten minutes, but had a fatal tendency to spar outside the off-stump. He was not a great defensive player, and an innings of his was likely only to have two outcomes. He had a spectacular head of hair [*natural, incidentally, unlike some players of that period*] and was a whiz at chatting up the bimbos. He enjoyed scoring heavily, but gave the impression that he preferred knocking back the wine [*but only the best*]. He did not seem to make much effort, but that was because of his horizontal technique.

We also had an all-rounder, who was a bit over the top. He scored wherever cricket was played, nudge-nudge, wink-wink. He knew all about travel, know-what-I-mean? He had an unfortunate haircut and wasted his time playing moronic games. He played his best stuff years ago, but still seemed to enjoy himself. He left his cricket in the lap of the gods, and knew a thing or two about dancing, nod's-as-good-as-a-wink-to-a-blind-batsman, eh?

We had a fast bowler who was a bit of a gloomy old person. He was capable of doing remarkable things, but always looked as if he was stoned out of his mind when he was doing them. His run-up was distinctly odd, and he always looked as if he had no idea whether it was arseholes or Tuesday.

We also had a spinner, who was a bit of an oddball. He was good at bowling, and some twit paid him quite a lot of money to wear a plastic watch when he was playing. He loved trouble, and picked fights with his captains. He had a brilliant and talented wife, and as further evidence of good sense, he chose a mighty man to write his biography. [*This is an in-joke.*]

And so we all set off to watch cricket for the next five days.

Marshall

TED HUGHES

A Legend

Black was the without arm
Black the within heart
Black was the skin
Black the bouncer-dealing heart
Unable to reflect
The white light of pity.

Black were the entrails
Black the muscles and the lungs
Black the whiplash shoulders
Striving to put out the light,
Black the thought that propelled the blood
Red life seeking missile
Life seeking
Life seeking
            emptiness.

Lineage

In the beginning was the Ball
Who begat Bruise
Who begat Blood
Who begat Bone
Who begat Brain Damage
Who begat Bouncer
Who begat Pain
Who begat Victory
Who begat Rib-ball
Who begat Throat-ball
Who begat Head-ball
Who begat Fear
Fear Fear Fear

Bowling for blood
Wickets retirements
Anything

Trembling between striker and stricken
In the filth of an underprepared track

Marshall's Examination at the Pavilion Door

Who owns these rooted feet? *Bouncer.*
Who owns that backward shuffle to square leg?
    Bouncer.
Who owns these leg-guards? *Bouncer.*
The arm-guards, thigh-pads and rib-protector?
    Bouncer.
Who owns the helmet? *Bouncer.*
Who owns the fear inside the helmet? *Bouncer.*
Who owns the swaying? *Bouncer.*
Who owns the ducking of the rising ball? *Bouncer.*
Who owns the ducking of the ball that never rises?
    Bouncer.
Who owns the fear of the yorker? *Bouncer.*
Who owns the panic outside off-stump? *Bouncer.*
Who is stronger than desire for victory? *Bouncer.*
Who is stronger than all cricket?
Me, evidently.

Pass, Marshall.

Marshall Takes a Wicket

Moving stiffly under pads and helmet,
Moving stiffly under the weight of protection
Moving awkwardly because of Fear
Moving awkwardly because of the weight of Fear
Old Opener took guard.
                              (Marshall stood.)

Two legs
Demanded Old Opener
And willed his own to obedience
To move into line
And not to shuffle towards square leg.
                              (Marshall waited.)

Life stabbed through him
A dream flash
Of hopes dismayed
Smashed
Into constituent atoms
By the bouncers of the past.
                              (Marshall began to run.)

In a bowel-emptying silence
The weight of fear in his gut
Fear of pain
Fear of failure
Fear of Fear.
                              (Marshall bowled.)

Old Opener
Saw the ball leave the hand
Smash into the rubbish of the earth
He managed to hear, faint and far – 'It's the
    bouncer'
Then everything went
Black.

Screwtape On Cricket

C. S. LEWIS

My dear Wormwood,

I am delighted to learn that your patient has become a professional cricketer. Beware of congratulating yourself too soon, however: the Enemy is capable of using cricket (as he is everything else, in that vile promiscuous way of his) as a way to his house. But professional cricketers who are strong in his service are rare indeed: remember the eye of the needle in the Enemy's story. Legions of cricketers are already safe with Our Father Below.

You write somewhat intemperately of your success in tempting him to bouts of prolonged self-absorption, and the pursuit of his own ends. This is all very well as far as it goes. Such things are easy game where any professional sportsman is involved. But are you not aware of the dangers of all this? Self-absorption can lead to self-examination, and that brings the Enemy to his side at once. If self-appraisal should lead to an honest assessment of his own worth, we are in serious trouble. A sportsman is always faced with his obvious personal inadequacies, and this can lead to the very kind of self-awareness that we are most anxious to avoid.

You speak of his obsession with his personal performance, but even here we are not on safe ground.
The pursuit of excellence, even in so frivolous an
activity as hitting a ball with a bat, is full of dangers for
us. In that revolting and unfair way of his, the Enemy
has made excellence its own reward. If we are not
careful, the pursuit of excellence can subtly become
the pursuit of the Enemy himself. And that will never
do.

Seek to distract him with jargon. Our servants in
the newspaper industry have worked wonders here.
Do not let him assess the real value of his innings. Let
him think of it as 'classy' or 'swashbuckling'. Best of
all, let him think of it as 'professional'. The use of this
word is one of the really solid triumphs of our seman-
tics department in the past twenty-five years.

His relationship with his captain sounds promising.
Here, again, your technique must be to keep him
fuddled. On no account must he be permitted to think
about what he is doing. The captain clearly tries his
patience, and yet expediency dictates that he must
keep on his right side. It should not be too difficult to
obtain the result you desire: soon you will have him
behaving with grovelling self-serving sycophancy,
while fancying himself a saint for doing so. This is
what humans call eating your cake and having it, and
as a junior tempter you will have incomparable joy if
you pull it off.

You write with some enthusiasm about the opport-
unities for drunkenness and unchastity. Here you
betray your own inexperience as a tempter. These sins
are less useful to us than is often thought. But what

you have here is a matchless opportunity to invert the Enemy's valuation. Though he may not sin spectacularly in areas of drinking or sex, you can still use both these things for moral subversion – with the added advantage that he obtains no pleasure from the activities at all.

Your task is not to have him chasing women, or drinking a great amount. Instead, have him see these things as morally good. Have him see drinkers and womanisers as heroes. Try the word 'character' on him. You will have him paying lip-service to every kind of vileness and debauchery, while enjoying none of it himself, with no consequent pleasures and no dangers of remorse. He will not even be aware of the danger he is in. Thus we will bring him, smiling with vague companionability, down to Our Father Below!

There are problems in the constant playing of team games, of course. Anything that involves the sinking of self into a common cause is fraught with perils to us. Such activities can lead him to triumph and consequent thankfulness. Thankfulness, even when not specifically directed to the Enemy, can be disastrous to us. Failure can lead to humility and the urge for self-improvement. The artificial tensions of sport can even lead the most ungodly man to something very like prayer, and that must be avoided at all costs.

But a moderately efficient tempter should have a great deal of profitable amusement with a professional cricketer. If he uses his material wisely, he will soon be able to turn brotherhood into conspiracy, rejoicing into gloating, humility into resentment, and the pursuit of excellence into the kind of self-serving and self-deluding approach to his work that will carry over into everything he does throughout his life until he ends up safe and sound in Our Father's House.

Your affectionate uncle,
Screwtape

The Tragedy of Prince Botham: Part Two

WILLIAM SHAKESPEARE

DRAMATIS PERSONAE

THE KING OF ENGLAND
Of the king's party:
THE EARL OF MIDDLESEX
LORD ESSEX
LORD WARWICK
LORD LEICESTER
Of the rebels' party:
LORD DUNCAN FEARNLEY OF WORCESTER
IAN HOTSPUR, PRINCE OF BOTH
SIR PICCA, KNIGHT OF DILLEY
Others:
PRINCE VIVIAN THE MOOR
SERGEANT
PORTER
PAGE
MESSENGER
FIRST CLOWN
SECOND CLOWN
CHORUS

Enter CHORUS.

CHORUS: Oh! For a pace like fire
    That would behead the mightiest batsman
    To oppose us! Batters who could bat
    Bowlers to bowl, one captain to bestride
    The noble game! Then would mighty
      England,
    Like itself, rekindle frozen ashes
    And blaze in glory with a phoenix flame!
    Return with us now to those thrilling days
    Of yesteryear: English cricket rides again!

ACT ONE

SCENE ONE

Enter the KING OF ENGLAND.

KING: Who keeps the gate here? Ho!
    (*The* PORTER *opens the gate*.)
           Where is my Lord
    Of Middlesex?
PORTER: Hast thou a ticket?
KING: The King of England doth attend
    The Earl of Middlesex. Bring me to him now.
PORTER: By the mass, 'tis more than my job's
      worth.
    I see no ticket, and I see no tie
    About thy neck. Thou mayst not enter in.
KING: Thou addle-pated coxcomb, 'tis just not
      done

    To wear a tie when with a doublet
    One is clad! Beside, I am your king.
PORTER: 'Tis what they all do say. If I let one
    Come in, I'll have them all in here for sure.
KING: Thou weariest me!
    (*Draws sword and smites* PORTER.)
PORTER: Oh, I am slain!
KING: Now 'twixt these portals I can pass right
       through.
    Oh! That was something I have always longed
       to do!

ACT TWO

SCENE ONE

Enter MIDDLESEX *and* PAGE.

PAGE: The King of England is without.
    (Enter KING.)
MIDDLESEX: You are welcome, sire, to Lord's.
    (*Aside*) Goats and googlies!
KING: 'Tis not as king, but as a supplicant
    I come before your Grace. I need your aid.
MIDDLESEX: Speak! What is all this? Is England
       fall'n again?
    I see a strange confession in thine eyes,
    And if those orbs could speak, a tale of woe
    Dishonour and defeat should then assail me.
    Have we not captains in the field enough
    To scheme, dismay and thus o'erwhelm our
       foes?

KING: Lord Duncan, Earl of Worcester, with a
    rebel host
    Is on the march. Now, seeking to o'erthrow
    ourself
    He comes to Lord's as champion meaning to
    depart
    As king. They flock towards his spreading
    banner,
    And from every part of England and the world
    They seek to aid him. From Kent they come,
    And e'en from loyal Somerset they follow.
    Now Duncan casts his net across the seas
    On to the shore of far-flung Afric
    And in its folds he finds a paragon
    Of batsmanship. Defiance stirs them all.
    Ian Hotspur, who the Prince of Both is called
    Doth boast in finest fustian, claiming
    To outshine the very sun in glory.
    Sir Picca, knight of Dilley, in his company
    By day and night doth swear he will be fit,
    And with a single ball will have my head.
    These rebels and their most unruly earl
    Must be snuffed out!

MIDDLESEX: It shall be so.
    Do thou call together the mightiest men
    That English cricket can produce, and put
    them
    Under thy captaincy. Let us unfurl the banner
    With its red and yellow stripes and we shall
    make
    The name Mary le Bon ring out full loud.
    Then shall rebels tremble, and be put to flight.

Ah! English cricket! Thou used to be so great.
Thou art descended to a dreadful state!

ACT THREE

SCENE ONE

Enter DUNCAN, PRINCE BOTH, SIR PICCA *and other rebels.*

DUNCAN: Friends: we are gathered all together,
    And now, one mighty team, we shall advance.
    Our preparations are in order set,
    And so, these three days hence, I mean to be
    King of England. A sun shall rise in the
        firmament
    That shall not set while yet I live.
PRINCE BOTH: (*Aside*) I have been too much i' the
    Sun. Ha!
DUNCAN: My brothers, gather round. Sir Picca,
    Thou art ever in my thoughts, and tomorrow,
    An thou pass a fitness test, shalt bowl.
    In the van of our great army thou shalt go.
    See thou bowlest to the King: he fears thine
    arm.
SIR PICCA: The King! What is a king when he is
    faced
    By the ball he cannot play? What boots a
    crown
    When a ball shall cobra-like strike up
    From goodly length and strike it off?
    Such venom as did never humble snake

With his sharp fang impart, I'll conjure by my
    skills.
A king, thou sayst? Why then I'll crown him.
I'll send a ball with all my strength
To strike the very seat of reason, split his
    helmet,
Spill his blood across a blasted pitch!
King of England? Ha! Thou shalt see
That with this arm I'll crown him King of
    Hell!

DUNCAN: Why, there's my Picca! My friends,
    good rebels all,
Let us away.
(*Exeunt all save* PRINCE BOTH.)

PRINCE BOTH: To play or not to play: that is the
    question.
Whether 'tis nobler in the mind to suffer
The blows and bouncers of outrageous fortune
Or to take up arms against an over of troubles
And by hooking, end them. Duncan, prince?
Fearnley, king? My lord of Worcester soon to
    be
The King of England and I to aid him?
I that on the field of Heading Lee
And thrice again, and thrice times thrice once
    more
Did earn the right, if any man e'er did
To wear such garlands as a victor should!
Dare I then to wear that gilded garland
Which the noble brow of England doth adorn?
Or shall I settle for a pauper's prize:
The thanks, the smile, and the forgetting

Of a treacherous king? Oh vengeance!
As rebel I do stand before the world;
A greater rebel am I in my heart!
I shall cheat on cheating. I shall treachery
   betray,
Murder murderers and I shall rebel
Against rebellion. So shall I advance
In holy blasphemy and in villainy
Most noble.
Soon the watching world will have its king!
Ian Hotspur, mighty Botham, shall be king!

SCENE TWO

Enter FIRST CLOWN *and* SECOND CLOWN.

FIRST CLOWN: By the mass, the pitch is passing
   quick.
SECOND CLOWN: And yet 'tis somewhat slow.
FIRST CLOWN: By the mass, 'tis slow as well! Aye,
   marry and God's sonties, know you what I
   have here?
SECOND CLOWN: I cannot tell.
FIRST CLOWN: 'Tis not of mine, yet 'tis mine. 'Tis
   not of thine, thou knowst not of't, and yet 'tis
   thine as well as mine. 'Tis a cake from Mrs
   Ada Cramp of 3, Ironside Crescent,
   Scunthorpe, and passing good it is, I'll
   warrant. Thanks to thee, kind mistress, if
   th'art listening in.

SECOND CLOWN: She listens e'en in a French
    tailor's hose, if she talks not in the nose, i' the
    Italian fashion.

FIRST CLOWN: Thou saucy knave, I cannot
    understand thy banter.

SECOND CLOWN: Nor I, by'r Lady. I tell thee, I
    understand not what goeth off out there. In
    my day, happen and any road up, we knew
    how to play the game, unlike the varlets of
    today. I tell thee, and that right warmly,
    cricket, 'tis a sideways game!

FIRST CLOWN: Thou slayest me with thy wit.

ACT FOUR

SCENE ONE

Enter KING, MIDDLESEX *and followers.*

KING: Now are my noble friends all gathered here
    To guard the holy place Mary le Bon.
    From every end of England you arrive
    And now proud Worcester, hearing of your
        coming,
    Doth taste his fear and doubt his own
        ambition.
    My lord of Essex and your grace of Warwick,
    You are especially welcome here beside us.

ESSEX and WARWICK: In this and all things we
    shall serve Your Majesty.

KING: And do I see my lord of Leicester
    Skulking in the backward ranks as if he were

A common soldier? Good Leicester, I pray
　　thee,
Step forward that I might embrace thee now.
LEICESTER: I am ready to bat for Your Majesty.
KING: Ready to bat! Then mark thou this, good
　　friend.
Play the ball, I pray you, trippingly
Along the ground. Do not saw the air
With your bat, or with your usual airy grace
Waft speculatingly by off-most stump.
Play not across the line. I would as lief
The village blacksmith smote the ball for me.
Oh, it offends me to my soul to see
When one-day shots are played in what is sure
To be a three-day war. But who comes here?
(*Enter a* MESSENGER.)
MESSENGER: The rebel host with Worcester at its
　　head
Is even now upon us. From off the moat away
They pour, and now in very London
Make their stand. Defiance is their banner
And they now declare that in a scant two days
All Lord's, and all of England, shall be theirs.
KING: Fie, thou naughty messenger!
　　(*Strikes him.*)
MESSENGER:　　　　I am dead!
KING: What rebel thinks to hold our kingly self?
Onward into battle, good my lords
If rebel dare to put our state to threat
Then state shall rise, and rebel sun shall set!

SCENE TWO

Enter SERGEANT *and* PRINCE VIVIAN *the Moor.*

VIVIAN: What is this place?
SERGEANT: England, my lord.
VIVIAN: Haply for I am black, and have not
    Such soft parts as cricketers of England
    Do possess, but I do see before me
    A land full ripe for plucking, reft by strife,
    Division and committees, with such a want of
      policy
    That every man believes himself a captain.
    So I mean to marshal mighty forces
    From the far Antilles, bring them hither,
    Then, like a band of starving foxes,
    Made by brutal hunger yet more fierce
    Than ever gentle nature had intended,
    Together storm that twitt'ring house of hens
    That English cricket is, and there we'll feast
    On dainty birds too dainty e'en to live.
    And thus shall I, Prince Vivian, make slaves
    Of those that made my fathers slaves before!

SCENE THREE

Enter CLOWNS.

FIRST CLOWN: Marry, 'tis a-raining.

SECOND CLOWN: That is no great matter, by the mass. Them that love us say the best bits always come when it be raining.

FIRST CLOWN: Dost thou remember that time when it rained on Michaelmas Eve some thirty year ago and more?

SECOND CLOWN: Nay, I cannot.

FIRST CLOWN: No more can I.

VOICE OFF: Thirty-three years.

FIRST CLOWN: Bearded friend, I thank thee. But tell me, arithmetician, dost think that because thou art virtuous, there will be no more cakes and tea?

SECOND CLOWN: Ale.

FIRST CLOWN: I don't mind if I do. Make it a firkin.

SECOND CLOWN: Thy wit doth murder me.

ACT FIVE

SCENE ONE

Enter DUNCAN *and followers*.

DUNCAN: There lies the field of St John's Wood
Where glory and a new-crowned king's remembrance
Waits for him that plays with majesty this day.
Prince Both, I charge thee, if you love me,
Guard my back throughout this threatening fight.

PRINCE BOTH: (*Aside*) Oh I'll do that, and with more majesty

Than thou shalt ever know, I'll play my game.

DUNCAN: Sir Picca, take this ball. 'Twas mine, 'tis
thine,
And now I'd have thee give it to the man
That stands and waits and doth desire it least.

SIR PICCA: Aim me, my lord, I am thine arrow,
The heart of all thy foes, my resting place.

DUNCAN: So short thy length, and at the throat
thy line!
Bowl swift and short, and England shall be
mine!

SCENE TWO

Enter lords of ESSEX *and of* WARWICK.

ESSEX: Let us stand, good friend and good my
lord.
To bat. With care and circumspection
We shall last this day.

WARWICK: With willing heart
I stand beside thee. To the foe we turn.
(*Enter* SIR PICCA.)

SIR PICCA: Ha! Have at you, openers whose folly
Is greater far than all their bravery.
(*They fight.*)

ESSEX: Oh! I am slain!

WARWICK: I join thee, friend, in death.

SIR PICCA: Thus two that in my path did stand
now lie.

But to my plan. Hotspur, Prince of Botham,
I mistrust, and think he plans to block
My road to glory. But that he'll not, by Jove,
Inside his Dundee cake I'll poison pour,
And inside him that cake will death despatch.
Thus perish those that do oppose Sir Picca!

SCENE THREE

Enter the lord of LEICESTER.

LEICESTER: The battle goes ill, and I beside my
    king
    Must make a stand – but who is this that
    comes?
    (*Enter* PRINCE BOTH.)
PRINCE BOTH: 'Tis I, Ian Hotspur, Prince of Both.
    Prepare to feel the weight of princely bat!
    (*They fight.*)
LEICESTER: I am dead.
PRINCE BOTH: So lies the Earl of Leicester. So
    stand I.
    Yet still I face a foe on either side,
    And so like Cerberus I go to fight.
    With one forward and one backward eye,
    I draw my plans. Sir Picca, ever loyal
    To rebel Worcester, shall rebel no more.
    I'll place these grains of venom in his tea
    And thus no team shall win this battle – only
    me!

SCENE FOUR

Enter KING.

KING: I go not to this battle for to fight
     With any serf that cares cross swords with me,
     More like a knight that ent'ring in the lists
     Does seek to fight the champion: him alone.
     Thus for his honour and his lady's grace,
     He will trade blows with no man save this
       one.
     Into the lists of battle now I come,
     And I not war, but single combat seek.
     Where art thou Duncan? Earl?
     (*Enter* DUNCAN OF WORCESTER.)
     Oh, saucy Worcester!★ Thinkest thou to hide
     From us, that are your royal king and lord?
DUNCAN: Have at you, king and lord of nothing,
     Thou master of a thousand fleeing subjects
     And general of an horizontal army.
     King of nowhere, lord of no man, fight!
     (*They fight.*)
KING: Oh, blasphemer, I am slain full dead.
     (*Enter* PRINCE BOTH.)
PRINCE BOTH: My lord, a king lies dead.
     Another stands in majesty before me.
     Your enemy is slain.
DUNCAN: And I the victor stand.

★ This joke was stolen from *Beyond the Fringe* and is
intended as an elegant expression of indebtedness to it.

PRINCE BOTH: Give me your royal hand.
> (*Takes hand.*)
>> And by this hand
> I'll slay thee now!

DUNCAN: Treachery! I die.

SCENE FIVE

Enter SIR PICCA *and* PRINCE BOTH.

SIR PICCA: Friend and noble prince, good Ian
> Hotspur,
> It seems that by our might we win this day.
> Let us drink our victory tea and eat with joy
> This ceremonial cake whose sweetness
> Shall the sour taste of sadness overcome.

PRINCE BOTH: I'm with thee, friend, my good Sir
> Picca.
> The prince carouses to thy glories.
> I eat this cake, a thankoff'ring to thee.

SIR PICCA: And now this cup of tea, I pledge to
> thee,
> My brother in arms this day.

PRINCE BOTH: As brother feasts with brother, let
> us drink.

SIR PICCA: Oh, I am slain!

PRINCE BOTH: Treachery feasts with treachery! I
> die!
> (*Enter* PRINCE VIVIAN.)

VIVIAN: What is this game that England plays?

Where are the cricketers of whom she boasts?
Look no more, unless thou seekst to learn
Of carnal, bloody, and unnatural cricket,
Casual dismissals, declarations mistook,
Accidental judgements and a summer
Packed with folly. England lies in ruins.
Carry out the dead. Commit them to the
    flames,
And when all England's cricket is consum'd
Sweep up the ashes, place them in an urn
And let four captains bear them, like a trophy,
To the stage. English cricket here lies dead,
And the verdict is accurs'd self-slaughter.
Now shall I march to triumph after triumph
After easy footling triumph. Go, bid the
    bowlers bowl.
(*Exeunt survivors, marching; after which a peal of
cricket balls is shot off.*)